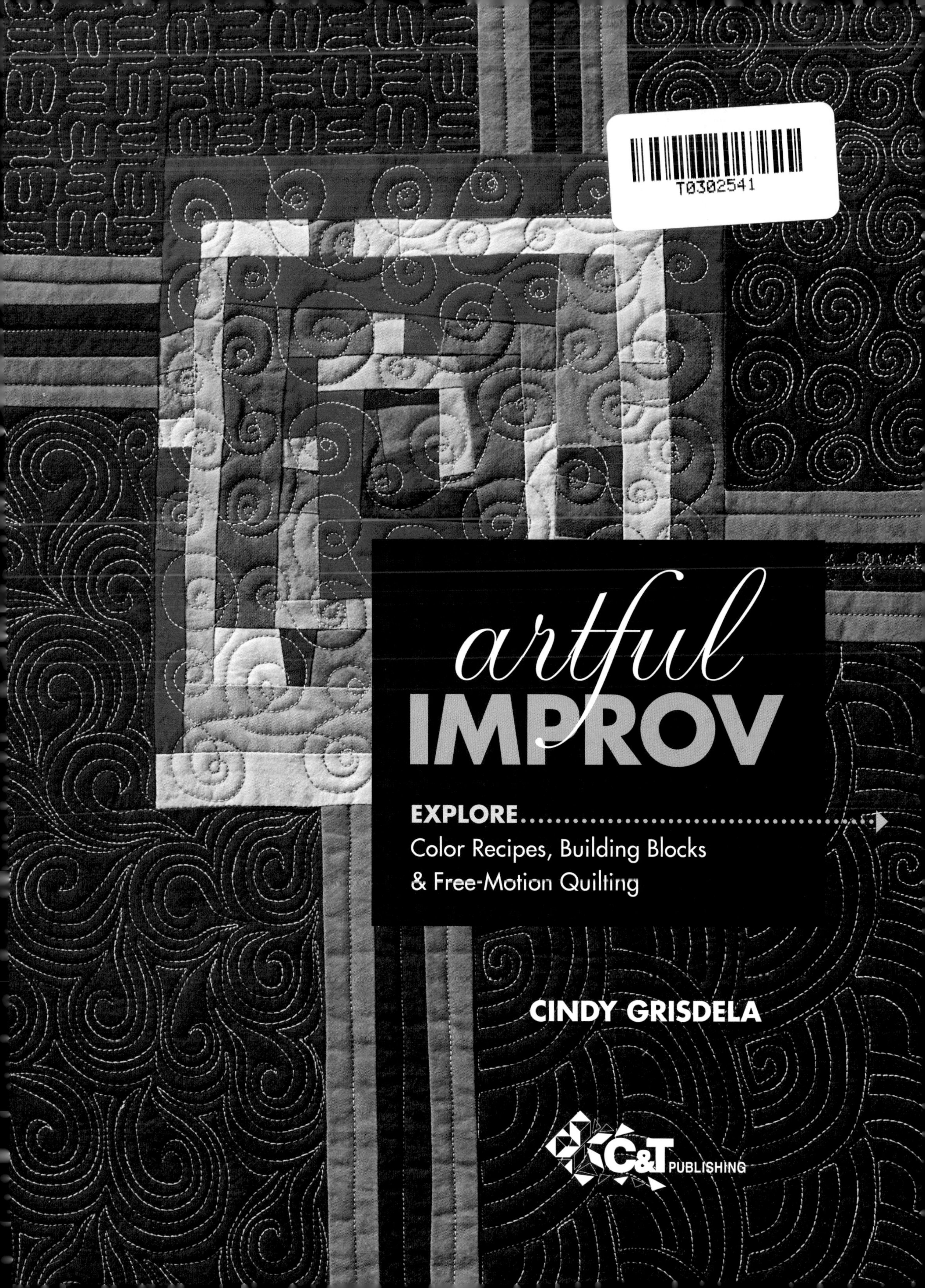

artful IMPROV

EXPLORE
Color Recipes, Building Blocks
& Free-Motion Quilting

CINDY GRISDELA

C&T PUBLISHING

Publisher: Amy Marson

Creative Director: Gailen Runge

Editor: Lynn Koolish

Technical Editor: Julie Waldman

Cover Designer: April Mostek

Book Designer: Christina Jarumay Fox

Production Coordinator: Tim Manibusan

Production Editor: Alice Mace Nakanishi

Illustrator: Aliza Shalit

Photo Assistant: Carly Jean Marin

Photography by Diane Pedersen, unless otherwise noted

Published by C&T Publishing, Inc., P.O. Box 1456, Lafayette, CA 94549

Library of Congress Cataloging-in-Publication Data

Names: Grisdela, Cindy, 1958- author.

Title: Artful improv : explore color recipes, building blocks & free-motion quilting / Cindy Grisdela.

Description: Lafayette, CA : C&T Publishing, [2016] | Includes bibliographical references.

Identifiers: LCCN 2016000613 | ISBN 9781617452611 (soft cover)

Subjects: LCSH: Quilting. | Patchwork--Patterns. | Patchwork quilts. | Improvisation in art.

Classification: LCC TT835 .G7654 2016 | DDC 746.46--dc23

LC record available at http://lccn.loc.gov/2016000613

Printed in Malaysia

10 9 8 7 6

dedication

With love and thanks to my parents, Ben and Eleanor Samuels, who gave me roots and wings and always encouraged me to fly.

acknowledgments

Many thanks to my mom, Eleanor, who taught me to sew all those years ago and has encouraged me all along the way. Much appreciation to my friends and fellow artists in Great Falls Studios, who provided a community of support as I took baby steps, and then larger ones, to become an artist. When I needed to spread my wings a little more, the opportunities provided by Studio Art Quilt Associates have been invaluable.

This book would not be a reality without the vision of my editor, Lynn Koolish, at C&T Publishing—thanks, Lynn.

I'm grateful to Karla at Cherrywood Fabrics and Heather at Superior Threads for providing fabric and thread for many of the projects in this book.

Thank you to my students who contributed work for the student section (page 68)—Pat Attkisson, Jeanne Coglianese, Donna Marcinkowski DeSoto, Libby Samuel, Michelle Stolte, and Gloria Warwick.

Finally, to my husband and sons—there aren't words to express my gratitude for your support, encouragement, and love. My son Phil read through the book multiple times and made it stronger. My son Matt gave me faith that it would all come together. And my husband, Phil, has pushed me, believed in me, and loved me for the last 30 years. You guys are the best!

contents

INTRODUCTION 4

HOW TO USE THIS BOOK 8

WHAT IS IMPROVISATION? 10

GETTING ORGANIZED 13
Sorting by Size and Color • What to Do with Scraps • Saving Leftovers

CREATING A COLOR RECIPE 16
The Color Wheel • Using a Color Recipe • Increasing Your Color Confidence

ELEMENTS AND PRINCIPLES OF DESIGN 24
Elements of Design • Principles of Design • Using the Elements and Principles of Design as You Work

WORKING IMPROVISATIONALLY 36
Creating a Design Wall • Auditioning Designs • Give It Time

BUILDING BLOCKS OF IMPROV DESIGN 42
Angled Stripes 43
Improv Circles 47
Improv Blocks 51
Curved Strips 56
Inset Strips 59

LEARNING TO LOVE NEGATIVE SPACE 63
Creating Balance • Adding Texture

PUTTING IT ALL TOGETHER 68
Student Gallery

QUILT AS DESIRED 76
Hand Stitching • Machine Stitching • A Word about Thread

FINISHING TOUCHES 89
To Bind or Not to Bind? • Facings • Dealing with Irregular Edges • Alternatives to Sleeve and Slat Hanging

ABOUT THE AUTHOR 95

RESOURCES 95

introduction

Creativity is play. The more you play, the more creative you become.

Red Totem
by Cindy Grisdela,
20″ × 42″, 2010

I'M CONVINCED THAT EVERYONE HAS THE ABILITY TO CREATE. SOMETIMES WE FORGET OUR CREATIVITY IN THE HUSTLE OF DAILY LIFE, BUT IT IS THERE WAITING FOR YOU WHEN YOU ARE READY TO GIVE IT SPACE TO GROW.

One of the secrets to being creative is giving yourself permission to play. It's okay to make mistakes while you're trying something new. In fact, if you aren't making mistakes, you probably aren't learning as much as you could. Above all, realize that you don't have to be perfect—you don't have to share every piece you make with the world, but you'll learn something even from (or especially from) the mistakes. Embrace them!

Most of us have to start at the beginning. I made my first quilt over 30 years ago, inspired by a picture in a magazine. Since my background was sewing clothes, I made a 4½″ × 4½″ template from cardboard for the squares. I carefully cut out all the fabrics with pinking shears, because that's how I'd always done it. Needless to say, getting an accurate ¼″ seam under those circumstances was a challenge! Since I knew how to sew already, I assumed that putting together a queen-size quilt for my first project would be a breeze. As you can imagine, it took me several years to piece the quilt on the machine and then quilt it by hand; but I proudly gave it to my husband as a wedding present, crooked stitches and all.

Fascinated by the colors of the fabrics and the textures of the stitches, I learned from my mistakes and continued making mostly traditional quilts for many years. One day it hit me that all the quilts on my walls and on my beds were someone else's designs. And I realized that it was important to me to create quilts that were uniquely mine. That was the beginning of my transition from traditional to contemporary art quilter.

This transition has been an evolutionary process for me, and it can be for you, too. I started out tweaking traditional designs to give them a more contemporary feel. *Butterfly Kisses* is based on the traditional Drunkard's Path pattern, but I used black-and-white batiks paired with a variety of yellow, peach, and orange fabrics to make it more modern. *Wild Geese in Flight* (page 6) takes a Flying Geese pattern and supersizes it in an asymmetrical composition, then adds texture with free-motion stitching.

Butterfly Kisses by Cindy Grisdela, 30″ × 30″, 2006

One of my first quilts made without a specific pattern

Wild Geese in Flight by Cindy Grisdela, 24″ × 34″, 2009

A variation on the traditional Flying Geese pattern with a contemporary feel

Give yourself time to explore ideas that resonate with you. Log Cabin designs have always fascinated me, and I have made a number of traditional ones over the years. If you look at my newer work, you'll see that I'm still playing with the Log Cabin idea, except that it has evolved into a contemporary improvisational design, often focused on one large block, as in *Red Totem* (page 4).

I hope you'll be able to take some of the ideas in this book and be inspired to create quilts that are your own, reflecting your own tastes, experiences, and personality.

Embrace your own creative spirit and enjoy the improvisational process.

My creative space

Photo by Dean Souleles

how to use this book

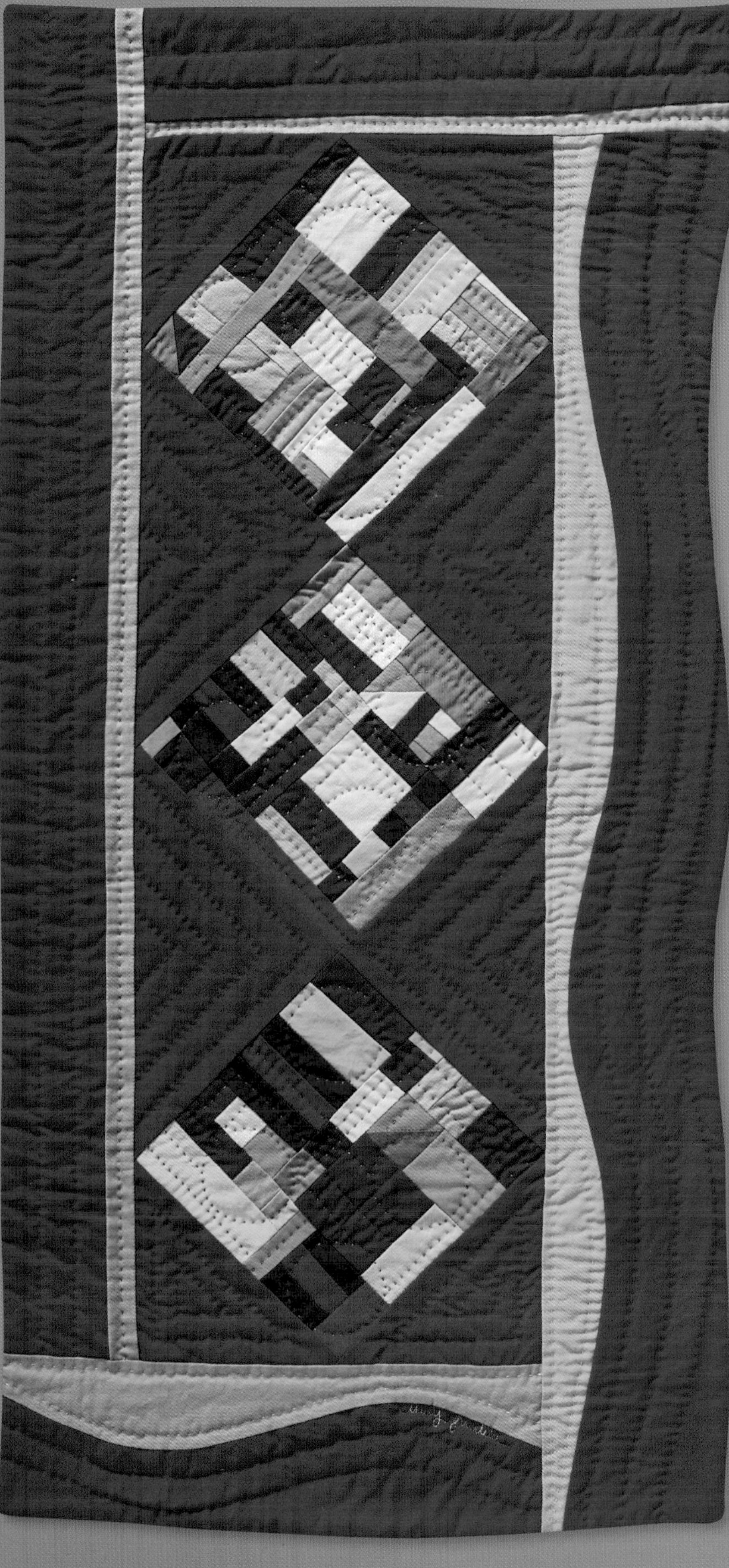

Red Hot Chili Pepper
by Cindy Grisdela
18″ × 37″, 2009

This quilt shows off Improv Blocks (page 51) set on point, bordered by curved strips and an irregular edge. A bright Anything Goes color recipe (page 22) is calmed by large areas of red that act as a resting place for the eye.

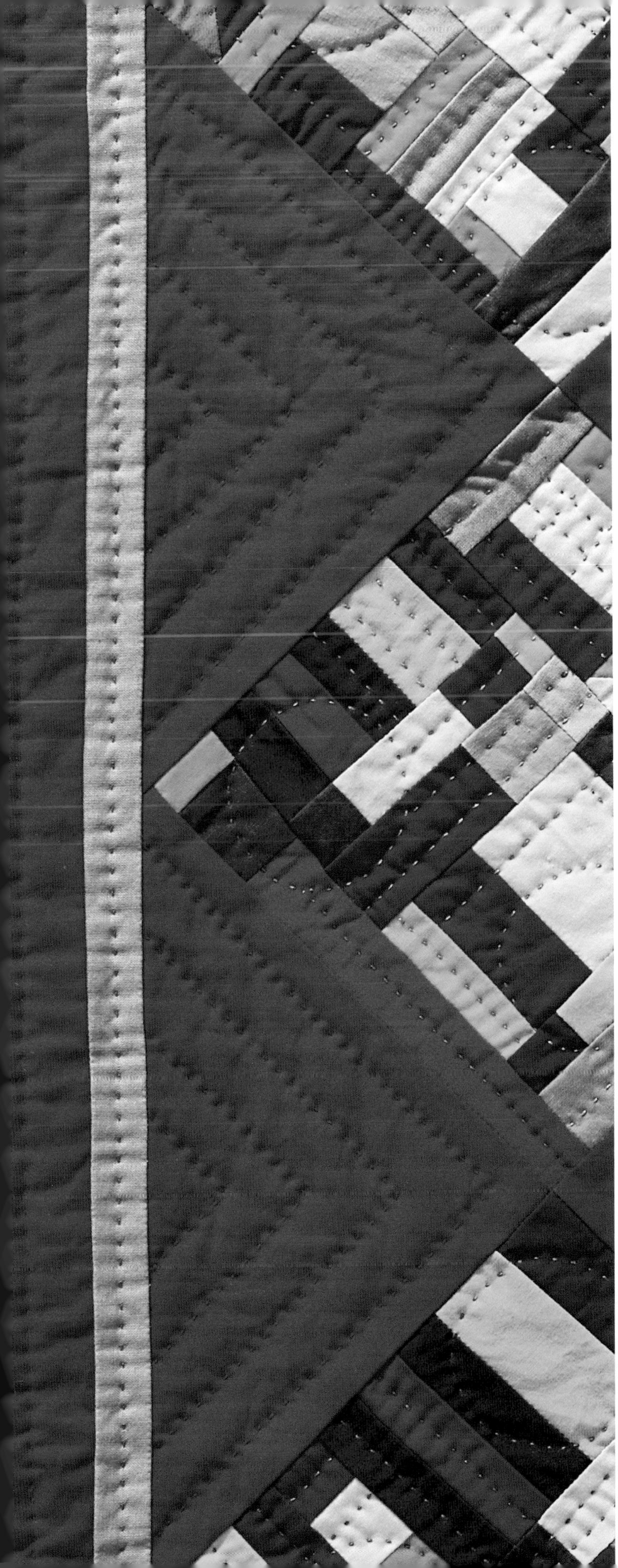

Use this book as a resource to help you tap into your own well of creativity and move on to the next level in your artistic journey—whatever that may be. With this book as a guide, you'll learn how to use simple design principles to create unique art quilts that reflect your own experiences. You'll feel empowered to let go of rigid rules and piece blocks in an intuitive, free-form fashion, using the basic principles of artistic design to create your own original quilts. Not using a pattern or precise measuring and cutting allows you to work spontaneously, painting with fabric as a painter uses paints on canvas, and then adding another layer of texture with free-motion stitching motifs.

This is a hands-on book—play with the exercises to expand your comfort zone and experiment. Don't expect to create a masterpiece the first time out. It's a little bit like learning the alphabet before you move on to reading. Don't worry about making mistakes; just have fun learning the vocabulary of improvisation.

Creating original quilts is fun and rewarding. Although this process may be most comfortable for intermediate and advanced quilters who are ready to move on from using someone else's patterns to creating their own designs, it is accessible to anyone who is comfortable using his or her sewing machine and rotary cutting tools.

what is IMPROVISATION?

Jazz Rhythms
by Cindy Grisdela,
35″ × 56″, 2009

This design is based on large Improv Blocks (page 51) in a riot of color with added energy from Angled Stripes (page 43). In this Anything Goes color recipe (page 22), large blocks of red calm the composition.

What is improvisation? How can you use it to create art?

Many people think of jazz music when they hear the word "improvisation," because of the talented musicians who created an art form based on making things up and performing on the spur of the moment, feeding off each other's energy.

Designing improvisational compositions in art quilting is a similar process. Start by picking out a piece of fabric or two and sewing them together. Maybe you like the colors together, or the shapes are intriguing. You don't know exactly what the final design will look like, and that's both exciting and a little scary. Usually I have a color recipe to start out with—maybe it's warm reds, oranges, and cinnamon browns. Or cool blues, greens, and purples. Once the process begins, each choice of color or shape influences the next. Try not to over-think each decision, but ask yourself if the colors are pleasing together and if the shapes you're creating are interesting. It's a little bit like putting together a jigsaw puzzle, but without the picture on the box. You get to decide what the finished design will look like.

Start an improv composition with just a few scraps.

tip

Don't throw away your scraps! Scraps and units discarded from another project might be just what you need for a new quilt. I keep my remnants and leftovers in a basket on my cutting area. Sometimes when I need inspiration, I'll take them out and look at them with fresh eyes. Maybe one of these small units will be just the thing to add an unexpected spark to a new design.

In the photo below, the striped unit on the far left side was cut from an earlier project. The angles on the green wedge lead the eye into the design and create lines that make the composition more interesting. While I normally avoid putting two pieces of the same color together, the orange in the stripe relates to the orange in the center and creates an entirely new shape. I like to call these intersections happy accidents that can't be planned out ahead of time. These unexpected twists often make the final design much more compelling than it would have been otherwise.

Build the design and let the colors and shapes evolve.

CONTROLLED CHAOS

You may ask, "How do you know when it's finished?" Because this is a no-rules process, you have to create your own guidelines to give structure to your project, such as the color recipe you're going to use or the size of the finished block. Whenever you aren't sure, you can use the principles of design (page 30) to evaluate your work as you create.

Remember that you aren't just throwing the kitchen sink at the design wall. *Jazz Rhythms* (page 10) is an example of a quilt that has a lot of activity and energy. But if you look closely, you'll see that there are rectangles of red strategically placed throughout the composition to give definition to the blocks. These pieces also provide resting places for the eye so the design isn't as overwhelming visually.

Some of these designs may look simple, like they just happened. But in reality they take quite a bit of time because the process can't be rushed—it has to evolve. Often I have to walk away or focus on another project in order to allow my brain to percolate through the options, and each design idea tends to build on the one before it.

This is the beauty of improvisational design—the give and take of a process in which each design decision (about color, line, or shape) influences the next one.

In the following chapters, you'll learn about the process in detail.

getting ORGANIZED

Photo by Dean Souleles

Wire baskets hold larger pieces of fabric.

Organizing your fabric is the first step in improvisational quilting. Fabric is the raw material of your art, just like paints or clay are raw materials for painters or sculptors. It doesn't matter how you go about putting your materials in order, just so you know where things are and how to find them easily. You don't want to lose precious time—when you could be creating—digging through your stash to find those great leftover strips you had out last week.

SORTING BY SIZE AND COLOR

There are a lot of ways to organize your fabric collection. You can separate your fabrics into type—solids, batiks, commercial prints, and hand dyes, for example. Then you could further sort them by color, or by scale—pieces with splashy large-scale designs in one container and small tone-on-tone prints in another. Maybe you have a large collection of hand-dyed or hand-printed fabrics and they need to be categorized further.

Each of us is unique, and each fabric collection is a reflection of our individual likes and dislikes. My fabric is organized roughly by color, by type of fabric (solids, batiks, printed commercial pieces), and by size. For the large pieces, I have wire baskets on runners set up on two sides of my studio. They are just the right height to allow my cutting surface to rest on top of one set and my ironing surface on the other. I've been quilting for more than 30 years, and I have a lot of fabric. Yardage goes in the wire baskets, folded into packets and placed on end so I can get as many pieces as possible in the basket and still see what's there. Any piece larger than about a fat eighth goes in there.

I have quite a bit of patterned fabric that I don't use much anymore for the fronts of my quilts, since I prefer using solid fabrics so my stitching will show better. It doesn't bother me to have that older stash though, because I use those pieces on the backs of quilts that are large enough to hang freely on the wall. It's like a secret that only I and the eventual purchaser of the piece know. Sometimes it surprises me when I make a pieced back using patterned fabric and someone tells me it should be a two-sided quilt!

Back of *Spice of Life* (page 65). The pieced back of this quilt uses patterned fabric from commercial prints in my stash.

WHAT TO DO WITH SCRAPS

Scraps are strips, strings, rectangles, squares, triangles, and leftover blocks. I keep strips and leftovers as small as 1″ wide. My scraps are organized in colorful small baskets that live on the top of my cutting surface. The baskets are sorted by color, with a separate basket for leftover blocks and sewn-together strips. It's up to you to decide how small is too small when it comes to keeping your scraps.

Photo by Cindy Grisdela

Colorful baskets hold scraps until needed.

Use whatever system makes sense to you. You could use plastic bins instead of baskets, or use whatever containers you have handy. Sometimes you will have more of one color than another, and you may need to break down your blues into light and dark, for example. Or your red basket might be overflowing and you need to set up a separate one for orange. The point is to be able to easily find what you have.

Saving Leftovers

What about the leftovers?

Leftovers can be blocks that didn't work, narrow strips that you cut to straighten an Angled Stripe set, Improv Circles whose colors weren't right, or curved pieced borders that were cut off to fit. Don't throw them away! These are the seeds of new ideas.

Basket of leftovers

Often I create planned leftovers, just as I might in cooking. If I'm working on Improv Blocks (page 51), Angled Stripes (page 43), or Curved Strips (page 56) for a project, I make a few extra ones so I have choices when I'm designing my composition. I toss those extras/leftovers into their own container so I'll know exactly where they are when I need them to jump-start my next design.

Time Travel (page 33) is an example of a quilt that grew from leftovers. I was experimenting with Angled Stripe blocks for another quilt, and I threw the trimmings from squaring up the blocks into the trash by my sewing table. When I glanced into the trash can later, I saw a colorful mess of leftover strips that I realized I couldn't bear to toss out. The Angled Stripes that were set into multicolored rectangles alternating with Improv Blocks in *Time Travel* came out of the trash!

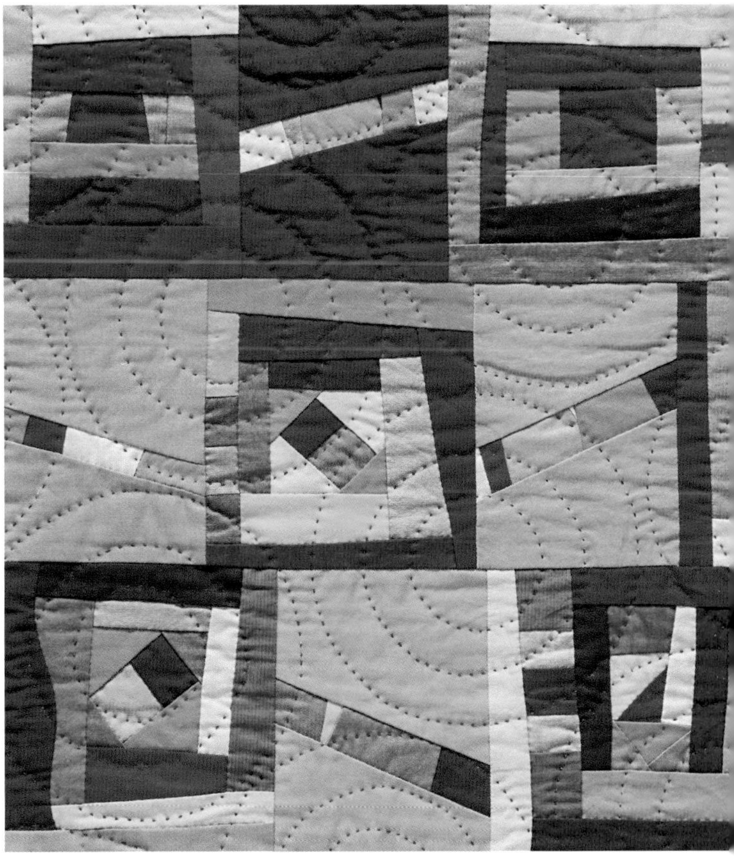

Detail of *Time Travel* (page 33). You never know when leftovers will turn into an entirely new design.

creating a COLOR RECIPE

Island Hopping by Cindy Grisdela, 28″ × 36″, 2014

This quilt incorporates a variety of blues and greens in an analogous (page 20) color scheme, plus a few accents of red and orange for contrast.

Color choice is very personal, and it's a decision that many quilters struggle with. I like to cook, and creating a color scheme for a quilt feels a lot like putting together a recipe. The basic structure of your design might be shades of red, from the fiery orange of a tomato, to deep burgundy, all the way to warm cinnamon. If you leave it at that, it might look fine but lack the zing that really makes the recipe special. For spice, you might throw in some contrast such as purple or a dash of lime green.

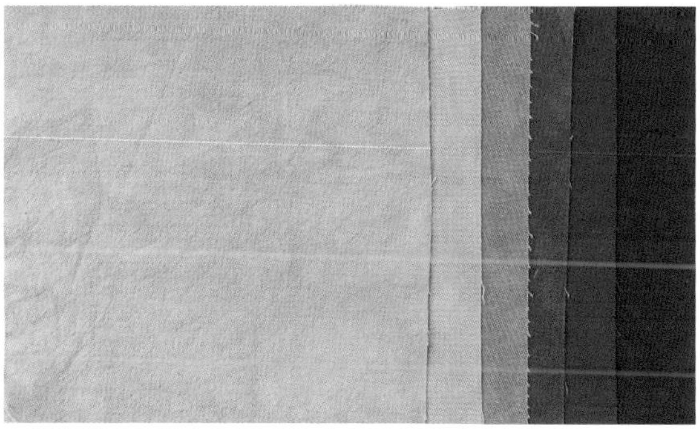

A variety of reds with a green for contrast

You've been putting colors together most of your life, even if you don't think of yourself as having an eye for color. All you need to do is look at the colors you wear and the colors you choose to live with in your home and you have a place to start. Begin where you feel most comfortable and let things evolve from there. For years my comfort zone was blue—sometimes edging over into the violet and red-violet range but rarely to the other side into greens. I made quite a few blue quilts before I was ready to move on to more adventurous combinations.

"How do you know if the colors go together?" is a question I hear fairly often.

My answer is that colors *don't* have to go together, at least in the sense that they don't have to match, and sometimes the composition is better if they don't. If you use a variety of greens in your design, ranging from bright lime to dusky olive, for instance, the eye will move around the quilt looking for connections, and that can make for a more interesting piece of art. *Island Hopping* (page 16) is a good example of this.

THE COLOR WHEEL

Color is one of the major elements of artistic design, and a color wheel is often useful in gaining a basic understanding of color.

There are three primary colors—red, blue, and yellow. Combining these colors gives you secondary colors. Red and blue make violet, blue and yellow make green, and yellow and red make orange. The other colors on the color wheel, called tertiary colors, are combinations of primary and secondary colors—red-violet, blue-green, and yellow-orange, for example.

Looking at the wheel, generally the colors on one side—yellow to orange to red—are considered warm. The colors on the other side—violet to blue to green—are thought of as cool. Warm colors tend to advance and lend energy to a design, while cool colors tend to recede and result in a calmer mood for the piece.

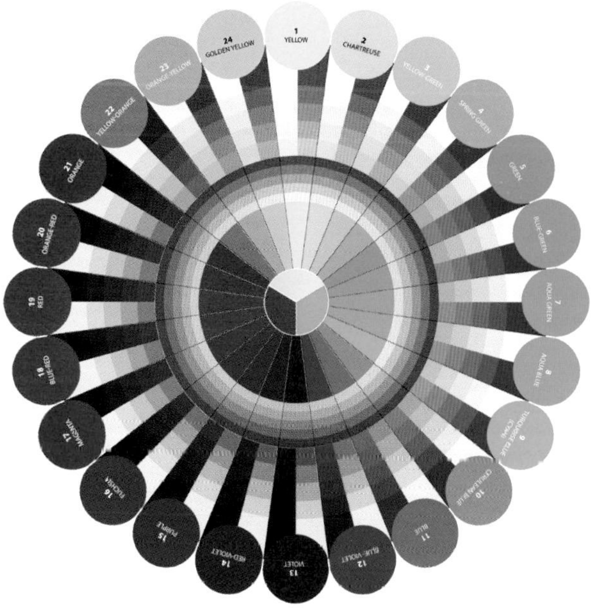

The Essential Color Wheel Companion by Joen Wolfrom (from C&T Publishing) can be a good starting point for using color.

tip

The Ultimate 3-in-1 Color Tool, the Studio Color Wheel, and now the Essential Color Wheel Companion, all by Joen Wolfrom (from C&T Publishing), are great color references.

For me, a design almost always starts with the color. I've been intrigued by how colors interact to create a mood or define a contrast since I was old enough to hold a crayon in my hand. You don't have to be an expert in the color wheel to create an effective art quilt, but it may help to understand some of the basics. And it's a great resource if you want to explore a new color recipe or you're stuck on a design you're working on.

A good starting point can be the tried-and-true color schemes—or color recipes, as I like to call them. There are many more color schemes than the ones presented on the following pages, but these will be enough to get you started if you are new to the color wheel.

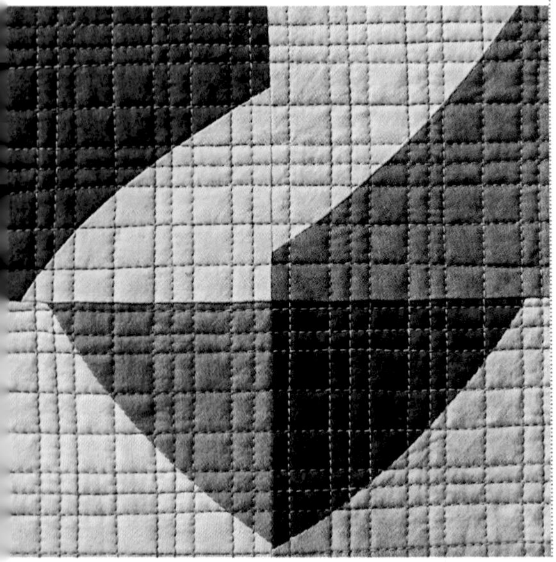

Monochromatic Color Recipe

In a monochromatic color scheme, all the fabrics come from one color family— green, for example. This is one of the easiest, most comfortable recipes to use because you just need light, medium, and dark fabrics in your chosen color family. A more formal way to think about it is tints, tones, and shades of the basic color, or hue (see Tints, Tones, and Shades, below). Monochromatic color recipes tend to be calm, soothing, and visually cohesive.

Tints, Tones, and Shades

Each color on the color wheel is known as a hue. If you add white to the hue, you get a lighter value, often a pastel, called a **tint**. If you add black to the hue, you get a **shade**, which is obviously darker than the original. And if you add both black and white to the hue, you get a **tone**, which is usually a softer, subtler variation of the color. A tone may be lighter or darker than the original hue.

Value

In the monochromatic color scheme the idea of **value** is particularly important. The value of a given fabric, whether it reads as light, dark, or medium, often depends on the value of the pieces surrounding it. Value is often more important than actual color in making a composition work, and using a variety of values is important in creating an interesting design, particularly with a monochromatic color recipe. In *Seahorses* (next page), I used a range of greens with different values, from deep hunter green to light pastel seafoam. In addition, there are some bluish-green shapes that push the green out toward blue on the color wheel, and some lime green ones that push out toward yellow on the other side. The contrasts keep the composition from becoming static and boring, which is often a risk with monochromatic color recipes.

Seahorses by Cindy Grisdela, 20″ × 20″, 2015

A monochromatic color recipe with a variety of greens

Analogous Color Recipe

Another color recipe that is comfortable to use, but usually more visually interesting, is known as analogous. This scheme uses colors that are close to each other on the color wheel, such as purple, blue, and green, or red, orange, and yellow. Often this recipe uses primarily two of the colors, say, blue and purple, with just an accent of the third one, green in the color run below.

Analogous color recipe with blue, purple, and green

Analogous color recipes are usually richer and more nuanced than monochromatic ones, with controlled harmony. See *Island Hopping* (page 16) and *Summer* (next page) for examples of analogous color schemes.

Complementary Color Recipe

Complementary colors are opposite each other on the color wheel—think yellow and violet, red and green, blue and orange. Quilts with this color recipe often have a very active, energetic feel because the colors really bounce off one another. If you feel there's too much energy, you can calm things down by using primarily one of the complements with just an accent of the other. *Cosmos* is mostly blue with accents of orange.

Photo by Greg R. Staley

Cosmos by Cindy Grisdela, 28″ × 47″, 2009

Complementary color scheme with blue and accents of orange

USING A COLOR RECIPE

Use one of these basic schemes as a starting place as you begin to design your art quilt. Ask yourself questions about what you hope to achieve with your piece. Is it a calm, meditative design? Perhaps a monochromatic or analogous recipe using cooler colors would be a good choice. Or is it more assertive? Then you might want to use an analogous scheme on the warm side with reds, oranges, and yellows, or a recipe using complementary colors.

Or maybe you just like purple and lime green together and want to start there and not think about it so much! That's an option too.

Adding the Spark

When you're using a controlled color scheme, such as a monochromatic or analogous recipe, there is a risk of creating a bland design. If your main color is red, try pushing it over to orange and also the other way, to red-purple. Also think about adding a spark to your composition in the form of a contrast to draw the eye in. In an overall warm scheme of red, orange, and yellow, for example, consider throwing in a splash of the complementary green to liven things up and keep the composition from feeling too static. *Summer* uses this type of composition.

Warm color recipe

Summer by Cindy Grisdela, 12″ × 15″, 2015

An analogous color recipe on the warm side with yellow, orange, and red, with an accent of complementary green for the spark

Anything Goes Recipe

There's also a place for what I call the Anything Goes color recipe. As the name implies, you can use any or all the colors of the rainbow with this one. The trick is to keep it from becoming overwhelming. The eye needs a place to rest. Usually we think of neutrals like ecru, beige, or taupe as offering the resting place in this type of design. But neutral doesn't have to be boring. In *Jazz Rhythms*, the red bands are the resting place in an otherwise energetic composition.

Jazz Rhythms by Cindy Grisdela, 35″ × 56″, 2009

An energetic Anything Goes color recipe

INCREASING YOUR COLOR CONFIDENCE

My approach to color is very intuitive. Usually I start with an idea of a color recipe to explore. I pull out all the fabrics in my stash that might work for that combination and then audition fabrics and shapes on the design wall until I get a design that sings. This takes some practice to do successfully, as well as a willingness to trust your instincts, but it works.

To increase your confidence with color, spend some time looking at art that strikes a chord in you, whether it's quilts, paintings, ceramics, clothing, or whatever. Take a thoughtful look at the colors surrounding you, from the crisp green of the lettuce in your salad to the deep purple of a pansy in your garden to the turquoise of your favorite blouse. Create a Pinterest board or a folder on your computer or a notebook with images that speak to you. Then look for common threads in your collection. Which color recipes make your heart soar? Identifying the color combinations that speak to you and playing with the exercises later in this book will help you gain confidence in your choices.

As an experiment, I created a series of small 12″ × 12″ quilts exploring color combinations that inspire me. They are all the same composition, just using different color recipes. I tried to include at least one that uses a recipe outside my comfort zone. It was interesting to see how each piece ended up with a slightly different feeling, just because the color choices were different. After you work through the exercises in this book, you might want to consider a similar experiment to help increase your color confidence.

Learn to trust your own color instincts. There's no "color police" to come and say you're doing it wrong. If it works for you, it works!

Photo by Greg R. Staley

Waterfall
by Cindy Grisdela,
12″ × 12″, 2014

Cool colors of blue and green

Photo by Greg R. Staley

Homefire
by Cindy Grisdela,
12″ × 12″, 2014

A complementary red and green color recipe

Photo by Greg R. Staley

Pueblo
by Cindy Grisdela,
12″ × 12″, 2014

A controlled recipe of warm reds and browns

elements AND PRINCIPLES OF DESIGN

Another Rhythm by Cindy Grisdela, 12″ × 12″, 2015

The vertical insets create upward motion, while the curved lines could represent a harmonious melody or the flowing of water.

Artists in every medium use the elements and principles of design to create and evaluate their compositions. Art quilters are no different.

It's important to remember that just because these designs are improvisational and embrace the "wonky" factor, you're not off the hook for crafting your compositions well. Many improvisational art quilts may look like they were put together randomly, and to some extent they are. But if you look closely, the best ones pay attention to the principles of art and design to enhance their success.

The following elements and principles aren't hard-and-fast rules; rather, they are intended only as guidelines to help you compose and evaluate your art quilt. But it's usually important to know what the rules are before you can break them successfully, if that's what you choose to do.

Note: *If you look up "elements and principles of design" on the Internet, you will find varying lists. The elements and principles listed below are the ones that I find most helpful.*

ELEMENTS OF DESIGN

The elements of design are the components or basic building blocks of the principles of design (page 30).

Line

Line is a visual path that provides a direction for the eye to move—horizontal, vertical, angled, or curved. It can also be the edge of a shape. You can see line in the fabric itself, in the pattern of a design, or in the stitching added to the final composition. Lines have their own qualities, depending on their direction. Horizontal lines can be calming, referencing the horizon. Vertical lines tend to have more energy, while diagonal lines are the most dynamic, conveying a sense of activity and direction. Curved lines can imply a more peaceful mood or rhythm.

In *Another Rhythm* (previous page), there are horizontal composition lines in the angled insets and vertical lines in the curved piecing. The insets themselves create strong vertical lines that convey upward motion. The stitching creates texture that amplifies those vertical lines in the background.

The composition of *Abstract Stripes* makes use of horizontal lines of different widths plus insets that are placed to create movement from one side of the piece to the other.

Photo by Greg R. Staley

Abstract Stripes by Cindy Grisdela, 13″ × 34″, 2010

Horizontal lines lend a tranquil feeling to the composition.

In *Summer*, insets in three horizontal lines imply a serene horizon—perhaps a sunrise or sunset, given the warm color recipe of yellow, orange, and red. But additional diagonal curved stitching lines add a dynamic element that activates the surface of the piece and changes the mood.

Summer
by Cindy Grisdela,
12″ × 15″, 2015

Curved diagonal stitched lines add unexpected energy to a horizontal line composition.

Shape

A shape is an area bounded by lines. It can be surrounded by straight lines—as in a rectangle, square, or triangle—or curved, as in a circle. In *Neighbors on the Square*, simple triangles, squares, and rectangles are put together to suggest house shapes. A dark triangle as a base with light triangles on the sides references the roof of the house, and the improvisational squares underneath imply the house itself.

Neighbors on the Square
by Cindy Grisdela,
16″ × 20″, 2011

Abstract house shapes are placed in the central part of the composition. The purple triangles set on top of squares bring to mind a child's drawing of a house.

The composition of *Captured Marbles* uses Improv Circles (page 47) as shapes to suggest marbles that you might have played with as a child. The circular shapes are bound by lines that seem to hold them in.

Color

Color is the hue the eye sees—red, yellow, blue, green, violet—and the value of the color, whether it's light, medium, or dark. Color varies in intensity from bright to dull, and in temperature from warm to cool. Color is perhaps the most important element in the art quilt medium. See Creating a Color Recipe (page 16).

Photo by Greg R. Staley

Captured Marbles by Cindy Grisdela, 16″ × 20″, 2011

Improv Circle units create organic shapes that are bounded by lines.

Texture

Texture is how the surface appears, for example, rough or smooth. You can create texture visually with the fabrics and elements you use, or actually with the stitching lines. The visually rich surface area of *Aztec Autumn* (page 51) is created with a busy combination of lines using Improv Blocks (page 51) and Angled Stripe (page 43) units. The varied heights and widths of the Angled Stripe units add to the impression of texture in the design.

Detail of *Aztec Autumn* (page 51). Surface texture is created by shape and stitching.

Red Zinnia is a simpler composition that has almost all its texture in the stitching lines. Each quadrant of the quilt has a different stitching motif—fans, swirls, and angular lines, for example.

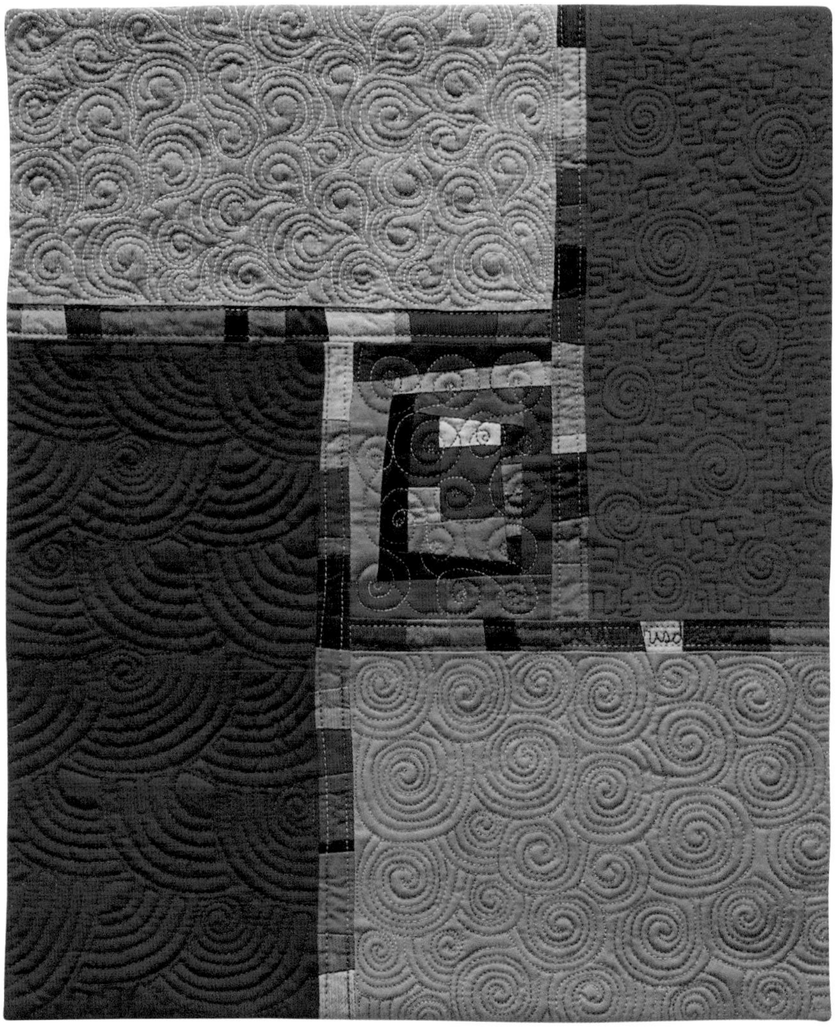

Red Zinnia
by Cindy Grisdela,
13″ × 16″, 2015

The texture is created in the stitching motifs.

In *Cosmos* (page 20), the texture is in the patterning of the batik fabrics used to create the design. There is texture in the stitching lines as well, but it takes a backseat to the lines of the patterned fabrics.

Photo by Greg R. Staley

Detail of *Cosmos* (page 20). The texture is in the pattern of the fabric.

PRINCIPLES OF DESIGN

The principles of design describe ways that the elements are used to create well-designed compositions.

Balance

Balance refers to the visual weight of the elements in a composition. It can be either symmetrical, where the elements on one side of the design are the same as the other side, or asymmetrical, where a larger element on one side is balanced by a grouping of smaller elements on the other. *Painted Desert* has an asymmetrical design in which the inset line at the bottom of the composition balances the large section of the design. In contrast, *Signs of Spring* has symmetrical balance, with a central focus block surrounded by borders and corner blocks of the same width.

Painted Desert
by Cindy Grisdela,
22″ × 26″, 2015

The balance in this composition is asymmetrical between the inset line at the bottom and the larger block in the center.

Signs of Spring
by Cindy Grisdela,
20″ × 20″, 2010

This quilt is an example of a symmetrically balanced composition.

Focus

Also known as focal point, focus is the area that the eye is drawn to as the main emphasis of a composition. Usually it's better not to have the focal point directly in the middle of a design, because you don't want to end up with a bull's-eye effect. Try mentally dividing the space into thirds either horizontally or vertically and placing the focal point along one of those lines. This trick is known as the rule of thirds. *Building Blocks* has its focal point in the right third of the quilt, while *Sunset Hills* has its focus in the bottom third.

Building Blocks
by Cindy Grisdela,
18″ × 22″, 2009

The focus of this composition lies along the right third of the quilt.

Sunset Hills
by Cindy Grisdela,
20″ × 20″, 2015

The focus of this composition is in the bottom third of the quilt.

Repetition

Repetition creates movement in a design, allowing the eye to move around the entire piece. There can be repetition of colors, lines, or any other element in the composition. In *Jazzberry II*, there is repetition in the three Improv Blocks (page 51), as well as in the light gray sections of curved piecing that draw the eye up and down the design. *Intersections* has repetition in the orange angled shapes and in the random Inset Strips (page 59) that help move the eye around the composition.

Jazzberry II
by Cindy Grisdela,
12″ × 24″, 2015

Repetition of Improv Blocks (page 51) and light gray shapes

Intersections
by Cindy Grisdela,
23″ × 37″, 2010

Repetition of shape and color for a dynamic design

Variety

Variety adds interest and keeps a design from becoming predictable. Vary the sizes of the elements you use and the distances between those elements. Consider using an odd number of units and add strips of different widths to bridge spaces between elements. *Time Travel* was composed in horizontal rows, so the blocks don't all match in size, but colors and shapes repeat so the design doesn't become too chaotic. The Inset Strips (page 59) are all set on different angles and point in different directions to add to the variety and help keep the design interesting.

Abstract Skyline has variety in the heights and widths of the vertical stripes, as well as in the different backgrounds. The spaces between the vertical stripes also vary in width, which adds interest to the design. The mostly analogous color recipe (page 20) and the repetition of shapes keep the design harmonious.

Time Travel
by Cindy Grisdela,
30″ × 34″, 2008

Variety is created by blocks that don't match.

Photo by Greg R. Staley

Abstract Skyline
by Cindy Grisdela,
24″ × 55″, 2010

Variety is created by the various heights and widths of the stripes and the different colored backgrounds.

Unity

Unity is the feeling that all the elements of a composition are working together so you end up with a harmonious whole.

In *Summer Breeze*, the Improv Blocks (page 51) provide both repetition and variety. The blocks themselves have an Anything Goes color recipe (page 22), but the yellow-orange background pulls the composition together in a visually cohesive way. An additional red-orange background behind the pieced part of the quilt helps pull the reds in the blocks forward.

Time Travel (page 33), is also a good example of a unified design. Repetition and variety in the individual blocks keep the eye moving around the composition. The activity in the Improv Blocks and angled insets is contained by the Curved Strip borders (page 56). The Anything Goes color recipe has a lot of energy, but the complementary red and green borders provide a resting place for the eye, even though they aren't neutral colors.

Photo by Greg R. Staley

Summer Breeze by Cindy Grisdela, 27″ × 33″, 2008

A unified design composition

USING THE ELEMENTS AND PRINCIPLES OF DESIGN AS YOU WORK

As you work through the process of creating improvisationally, you may come to a point where you feel something isn't quite right, but you may not know what it is. The following questions are very helpful in identifying what might be bothering you. These questions are also useful when you think you are finished with a piece—step back, take a look, and review the questions to see if you are really done.

QUESTIONS TO ASK

- Do I have interesting lines and shapes? Do they keep the eye moving around in the composition, or are they pointing outward? Do they convey the feeling I want to convey? (See Elements of Design, page 25.)
- Is there a clear color recipe? Have I added the spark? (See Creating a Color Recipe, page 16.)
- Is there visual balance in the design? Are there too many heavy dark colors on one side that draw the eye away? Are there light areas that create "holes" in the design? (See Give It Time, page 41.)
- Is there a clear focal point of interest? Have I given it enough space? (See Focus, page 31.)
- Is it too busy? Are there areas of calm that give the eye a place to rest? (See Controlled Chaos, page 12.)
- Is there repetition of colors or shapes that draws the eye around the design? Or is there an oddball that sticks out? (See Repetition, page 32.)
- Is there variety in the value and intensity of the colors and the size of the units, or are they all the same? (See Variety, page 33.)
- Is the design predictable, or is there an element of surprise and discovery for the viewer? (See Playing "What If?", page 38.)

Give the process time to evolve. Take a break or work on something else for a little while before coming back to look at what you have with fresh eyes. Often you'll see exactly what needs to come next.

working IMPROVISATIONALLY

Through the Window
by Cindy Grisdela
35″ × 19″, 2011

This quilt has several oddball red shapes that are outside the basic color recipe. The repetition of the red in several different areas encourages the eye to move around the composition looking for connections.

CREATING A DESIGN WALL

When you are working improvisationally, a design wall of some sort is essential. It can be as simple or as elaborate as you like. The design wall allows you to put up units on the vertical surface, step back and see how you like them, and rearrange them at will. You can even go away to have a sandwich and come back to see your work just where you left it (instead of having it redistributed by the cat, which is what used to happen to me when I used the floor or the bed as my design space).

When you're satisfied with your design, you can take the units to the sewing machine and put them together. Before I started using a design wall, I often got frustrated when I finished a quilt and hung it on the wall or put it on the bed and realized I should have pieced it differently. Or I got the quilt sewn together, sandwiched, and basted and had begun quilting before I realized there was a block in upside down.

A simple, portable design surface can be a piece of flannel or batting that you tack up to the wall with pushpins. When not in use, it can be taken down, rolled up, and put away. I used this method quite happily for years. Another easy solution, particularly if you tend to work on a smaller scale, is to cover an artist canvas with batting. In the studio outside my home that I share with a mixed-media painter, I have a 40″ × 48″ canvas covered with batting. I can stand it up on an easel when I'm there working and store it behind a table when the studio is being used for painting.

A simple, portable design wall made of batting-covered canvas

In my home studio, I now have a more formal design wall where I can create larger pieces. I bought 24″ × 24″ squares of foam insulation board from a home improvement store, covered them with batting, and taped the batting edges to the back with duct tape. I hung the squares in a 3 × 3 grid. If you want to have fewer joins in your wall, you can buy larger sections of insulation board. This may be particularly important if you do your own photography.

Formal design wall created from foam insulation board covered with batting

My wall is large enough that I can work on several pieces at once, which is a real benefit when working improvisationally. Sometimes ideas need to marinate for a period of time, and this setup allows me to spend that time making progress on another design. Often a new idea will pop into my head for the piece waiting on the design wall while I'm working on something else.

AUDITIONING DESIGNS

For many, the improvisational design process is intuitive. For example, I prefer not to sketch out my designs ahead of time, although if that process is helpful to you, by all means do it. I do make rough drawings of composition ideas that come to me when I'm not in my studio so I don't forget them later.

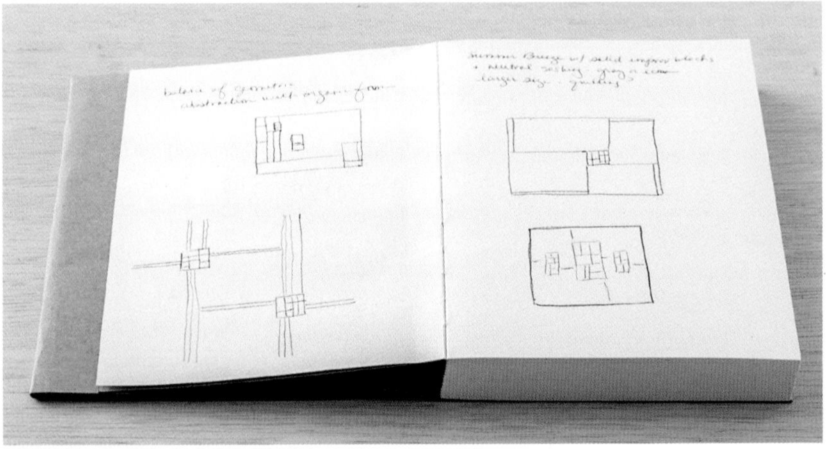

Rough sketches for composition ideas

While I often have a general idea in my mind of what I think the composition is going to look like, usually that's just a starting point, and my idea changes as I cut into the fabrics and create lines and shapes from the colors I'm working with.

As you design, it's a good idea to be thinking about what kind of stitching texture you might want to add when your quilt top is finished. Do you want the composition itself—the color, line, and shape of your design—to be the focus and the stitching to be secondary? Take a look at *Cosmos* (page 20) for an example of this type of quilt. Or do you want the texture of the stitching to be more central to your design? *Sunset Hills* (page 31) would not be as interesting without the texture of the stitching. Maybe somewhere in between is more comfortable for you. Give it some thought as you are creating your top.

Auditioning colors and shapes is an integral part of the process. My favorite question is "what if?" What if I add a different spark of color? What if I change the orientation of the units? What if I throw in another element (or two)?

Playing "What If?"

To give you an idea of what the improvisational process can look like, follow along with the creation of *A Little Citrus* (page 40). I started out with a cool color recipe of green (ranging from bright lime to almost olive) and blue (ranging from a rich royal blue to more subdued navy). Using those fabrics, I stitched together a set of Angled Stripe blocks (page 43).

Photo by Cindy Grisdela

Angled Stripe units (page 43) in a cool blue and green color recipe (page 16)

Auditioning the units on the design wall, I thought they seemed a bit too predictable. There's no element of surprise for the viewer. ***What if*** a dash of hot pink, the complementary color to the lime green, is added to liven things up a bit?

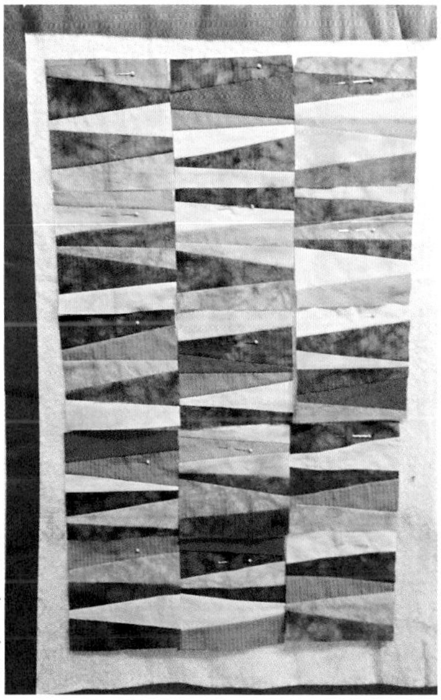

Photo by Cindy Grisdela

Angled Stripe units in cool colors with a dash of hot pink

That's definitely a step in the right direction. The pink adds punch and creates more movement to draw the eye around the composition. I like the lines created by the spiky Angled Stripes intersecting almost randomly, but I still want more energy. The primarily horizontal lines are too calm. ***What if*** I change the direction of the spiky units and make some vertical and some horizontal?

Photo by Cindy Grisdela

Angled Stripe units in a horizontal and vertical arrangement

tip

Use blue painter's tape to define the size of quilt you want to end up with. It gives you a reference point to start from and can always be adjusted later if needed.

Better. But the composition still isn't thrilling me. ***What if*** I add another element for contrast? And maybe another color?

Photo by Cindy Grisdela

Shake up the composition with Improv Circles (page 47) and a splash of orange.

Back at the sewing machine, I stitched up several sets of Improv Circles (page 47) using the blues and greens, with some orange as a complement to the blue in addition to the pink.

Now things are getting more interesting. The Improv Circle units are carefully placed to offset the spiky Angled Stripe units, making the whole composition more complex. And the splashes of orange and pink contribute repetition and movement to add to the visual appeal.

This composition has interesting lines and colors, and the shapes are unified and balanced (see Principles of Design, page 30). It could be finished and be perfectly fine. See *Hopscotch* (page 43) for an example of this type of composition. But ***what if*** I changed one more thing?

Using scraps from the previous units, I put together a section of Inset Strips (page 59), being careful to include some of the pink and orange for accent. Inserting the stripe section into the composition breaks up the symmetrical balance of the design, creating an element of surprise and a more complex composition.

You can play the "what if?" game almost indefinitely. It's a good idea to snap digital pictures of your design at each stage, so you can remember what you did earlier in case you want to go back to it. The photos also give you another way to evaluate the success of your composition as you move through the options. When you put the images up on a computer screen, or even just look at them on your mobile device, you will often see design flaws that weren't apparent when you were standing close to the design on the wall. This trick has saved me a lot of "unstitching," which is my least favorite part of the quilting process! Don't forget to use Questions to Ask (page 35) to evaluate your work as you go.

A Little Citrus by Cindy Grisdela, 25″ × 27″, 2015

GIVE IT TIME

Improvisation is not quick. It takes time for the best design to reveal itself. Each time you change an element of your composition, step back and evaluate. Take a photo and look at it on a screen. Walk away and do something else for a little while and see what you think when you come back to it. This is especially important when you aren't quite sure whether it's working or not, or you aren't sure what to do next. Use Questions to Ask (page 35).

Sometimes the digital photo will show you an oddball element or fabric in the mix. This might happen when you're using a wide variety of fabrics in your quilts because there are times when a fabric looks different when it's cut up than it did on the bolt. Or perhaps a color appears brighter or duller than it originally seemed when it's placed next to other colors in your design.

You have several choices when this happens. The easiest one might be to take the offending section out, and sometimes that is the best choice. But you might consider doing just the opposite and adding more of that fabric or color in another area of your composition. That can create movement, balance, and repetition that actually result in a better design (see Principles of Design, page 30). It may be just the spark you need.

Finally, if it's a color that seems out of place, you can replace that shape with another one that is a different value or hue, brighter or duller, lighter or darker.

As you let the design marinate, don't worry if there's a point where you want to just scrap the whole thing. That's completely normal in the improvisational process!

Engage in a dialogue with the emerging composition and ask yourself questions as you proceed. What do you like about what you have so far? What else does it need? Refer to Using the Elements and Principles of Design as You Work (page 35) to help formulate your questions. Is it unified and balanced? Is there a definite focal point? Is there movement and repetition of elements to keep the eye from stopping at any one point?

Try not to be in a hurry, and be open to the "aha" moment when it just feels right. It's hard to describe, and the moment will be different for everyone, but you'll know it when it happens! If it doesn't come right away, put the piece aside and work on something else. If all else fails, identify a section of the piece that you like, and focus on that. I struggled with one quilt for over a year before it became clear what it needed to become successful. I kept putting it up on the design wall and moving elements around, but they didn't click. It wasn't until I tried a completely different color idea that everything began to mesh and I was able to finish the piece.

Improvisation is by its very nature unpredictable. Go with the flow and enjoy the process.

building blocks OF IMPROV DESIGN

In this section, you'll learn five techniques to add to your improvisational toolbox. Some of them may be familiar, while others may be new to you. I suggest testing them out using scraps to see which ones you like best. You don't need to include every technique in every quilt!

If you would like to create units to incorporate into a small quilt top, start with a selection of warm colors (red, orange, yellow) and cool colors (blue, green, purple) in a variety of light, dark, and medium tones. *Or* try a selection of light, medium, and dark fabrics that you like together. Don't forget your scrap basket!

Strips and scraps of cotton fabric in solids—or fabrics that read as solids, such as tone-on-tone and small-scale prints—work best for these exercises. I usually avoid large-scale prints, but that's up to you. The greater the variety, the better.

Examples of building block techniques

You'll notice that I almost always use solid fabrics. I like solids because they seem more like paint to me. There's no secondary pattern to distract from the color, line, and shape of the design I'm creating. In addition, the texture of my stitching shows up much better on solids than it does on patterned fabric. But adding a few patterned fabrics into the mix can have interesting results. Don't be afraid to give it a try and see what you think.

My favorite fabric is solid, hand-dyed fabric from Cherrywood Fabrics. The fabric is richly colored and dyed so that it almost looks like suede.

Shot cottons will give a slightly different look. Kona Cotton from Robert Kaufman Fabrics works also, and it's less expensive when you're beginning to experiment with a new way of doing things.

ANGLED STRIPES

Hopscotch
by Cindy Grisdela
24″ × 24″, 2013

Quilt using Angled Stripe blocks and Improv Circles (page 47)

Angled Stripe blocks have many uses in improvisational art quilts. They can be used in a design on their own, combined with other blocks such as Improv Circles (page 47), or cut into narrow strips to add spark to a composition. I like to have a variety of these blocks on hand. The rectangles you start with can be any size, as long as the length is about 2″ more than the height to accommodate the seam allowances. The height of the rectangle should be about ½″ more than your planned block size before sewing.

MAKING ANGLED STRIPES

Sew all seams with the fabric right sides together using a ¼″ seam allowance; then press the seams to one side.

1. Decide on your color recipe (see Creating a Color Recipe, page 16). Select 6 fabrics, including 4 or 5 that coordinate and 1 or 2 that contrast for spark. For this example, I used a warm analogous color recipe of red and orange, plus complementary green and blue for contrast.

2. Cut 6 rectangles about 6″ × 8.″ Arrange the colors in a pleasing order. Consider alternating lighter colors or values with darker ones, so you don't end up with all your darks or all your lights in a row.

3. Stack the rectangles evenly, aligning the edges.

4. With the long sides on the top and bottom, use your rotary cutter and ruler to make 5 angled cuts through all the fabric layers, giving you 6 fabric stacks per set. Aim for a variety of widths with each cut, but make sure no piece is less than ¾″ wide.

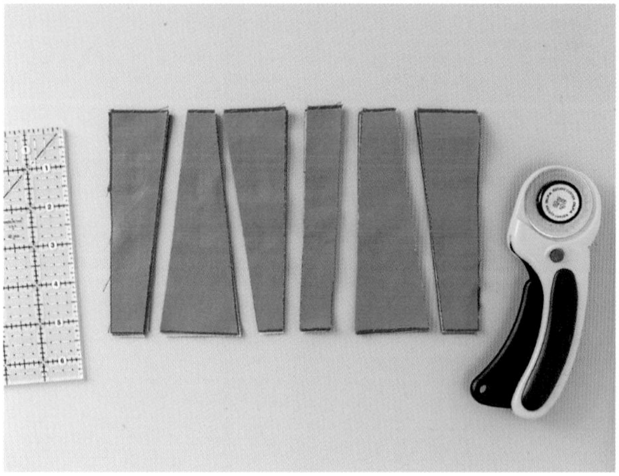

Stack and cut the fabrics.

5. Working from left to right, take the top piece of the first stack and move it to the bottom of the stack.

6. Take the top 2 pieces from the next stack to the right and put them on the bottom of that stack.

7. Take the top 3 pieces from the next stack to the right and put them on the bottom of that stack.

8. Take the top 4 pieces from the next stack to the right and put them on the bottom of that stack.

9. Take the top 5 pieces from the next stack to the right and put them on the bottom of that stack.

10. Leave the stack farthest to the right as is. You will have a different top fabric on each stack, and the colors in each stack will be shuffled.

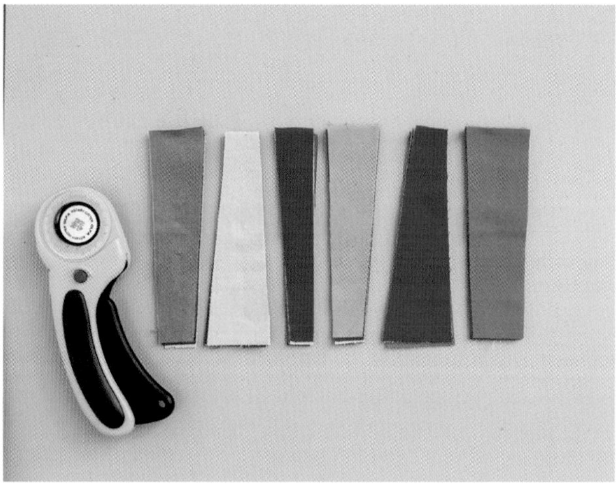

Rearrange the fabrics.

11. Starting on the left side, take the top pieces of fabric from the first 2 stacks and sew them together along their common edge. Take the new top pieces and continue chain sewing all the top pieces from those 2 stacks together so they will stay in order. Don't worry if the ends don't match exactly; they will be trimmed later.

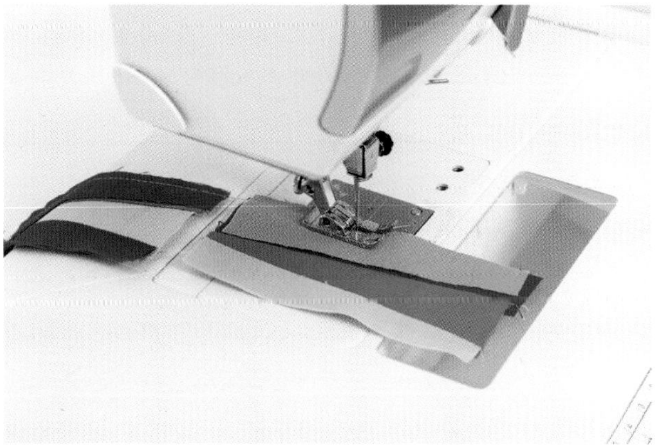

Chain stitch the strips together.

12. When all 6 pairs are sewn together, press the seams to one side, cut the thread between each pair, and restack the pieces in the order you sewed them.

13. Take the top fabric from the next stack to the right and sew it onto the first completed unit. Press the seam to one side when you are finished. Chain sew the rest of the pieces in the stack to your units from Step 12.

14. Continue adding the next piece in the sequence to the sewn units until you reach the last stack; then repeat until the units are all sewn. You now have 6 fabric units, with 1 of each of the 6 different colors in each unit. Trim the units to a uniform size.

Stitched and trimmed blocks

These units can be used as they are to create a design, or you can slice off narrow strips to use as details in other compositions.

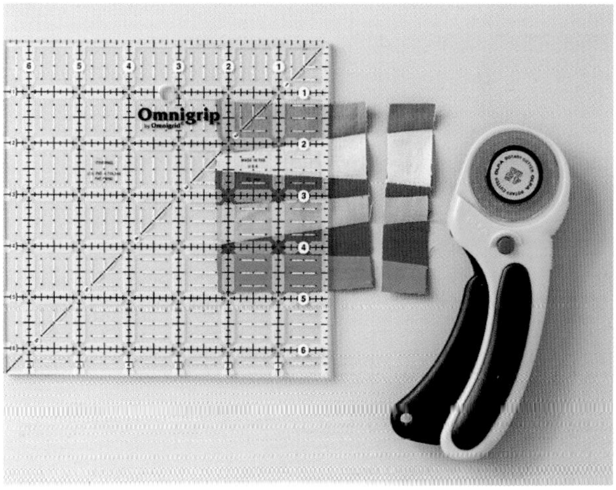

Narrow strips cut from Angled Stripe units are useful to add interesting detail to other designs. See Inset Strips (page 59).

Autumn Forest
by Cindy Grisdela
24″ × 32″, 2013

Quilt using Angled Stripe blocks and Curved Strips (page 56)

Blue Totem
by Cindy Grisdela
20″ × 36″, 2013

Narrow strips of Angled Stripe blocks add interest to an Improv Block (page 51) composition.

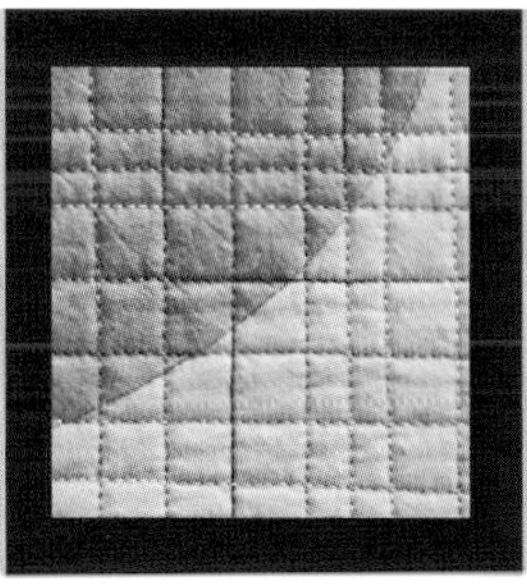

IMPROV CIRCLES

Box of Marbles
by Cindy Grisdela
16″ × 20″, 2011

The Improv Circle units in this quilt are arranged so they don't actually form circles.

Improv Circles are a modern variation on the traditional Drunkard's Path block. There's no need to fear curved piecing here—the edges aren't supposed to match. After sewing, you square up the blocks to the right size. To create your own blocks, cut the starting squares at least 1½″ larger than the desired finished size.

MAKING IMPROV CIRCLES

Sew all seams with the fabric right sides together using a ¼″ seam allowance; then press the seams toward the smaller arc.

1. Decide on your color recipe (see Creating a Color Recipe, page 16). Select 12 fabrics about 4½″ × 4½″ square. For this example, I used a double complementary color recipe of red and green and blue and orange in autumn tones. This will result in 3 Improv Circles, with 4 blocks each. If you want more or fewer, simply adjust the math so that you cut 4 squares for each block.

Pick your color recipe.

2. Arrange the squares into 6 pairs. The pattern works best if the pairs are different colors or different values of the same color.

Pair up the squares.

3. Align the edges of each pair and cut a gentle curve through both fabrics as shown, using a rotary cutter.

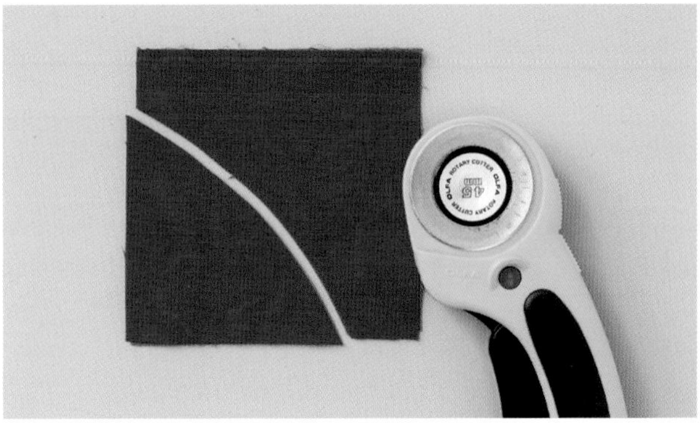

Align the edges and cut.

4. Separate the halves and lay out 2 new squares with a different color or value in each half. One piece will be convex, with the curve going outward on the edge opposite the point, and the other will be concave, with the curve going inward.

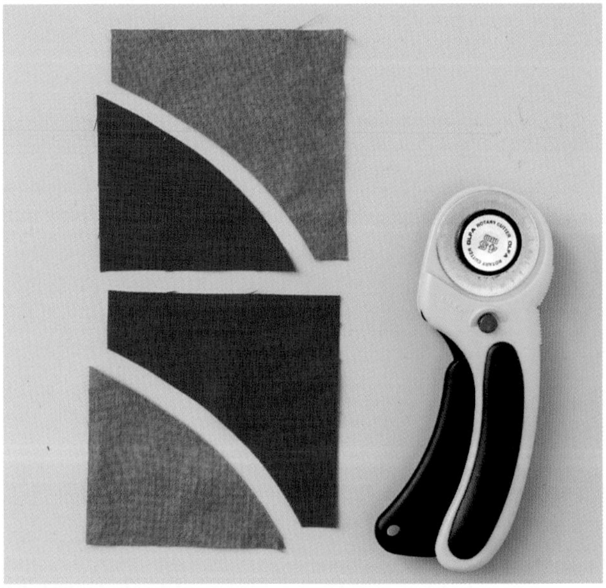

Separate the halves and rearrange the colors.

5. Sew the 2 halves together along the curved edge, with the concave piece on top, using a scant ¼″ seam. The edges will not match.

Sew the pieces together.

> *tip*
>
> You don't need to pin the curves for sewing. Simply align the beginning edges and stitch slowly, stopping when necessary to gently realign the edges. Don't worry if the seam allowance varies slightly. It will press out.

6. Press the seam toward the smaller arc.

7. Square up the block to 3½″ × 3½.″

8. Repeat for all the pairs. Try to cut each curve slightly different from the others.

9. Arrange the squares into blocks of 4, making a rough circular form.

Sew the squares into blocks.

> *tip*
>
> To maintain the different curves you cut, square up each block from the small section first.
>
> 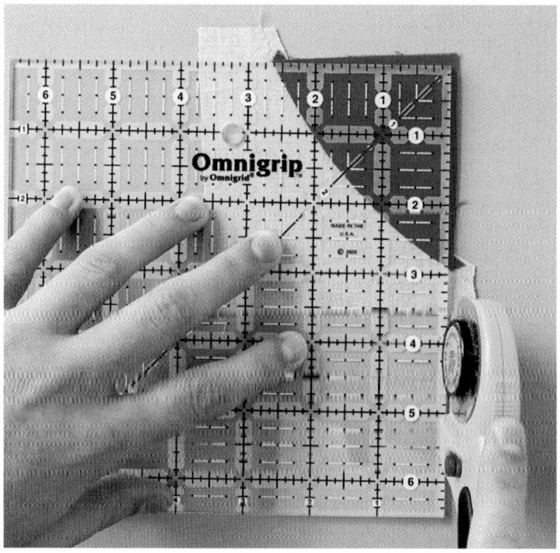
>
>
> **Trim.**

Photo by Greg R. Staley

Captured Marbles by Cindy Grisdela, 16″ × 20″, 2011

Made using two Improv Circle units

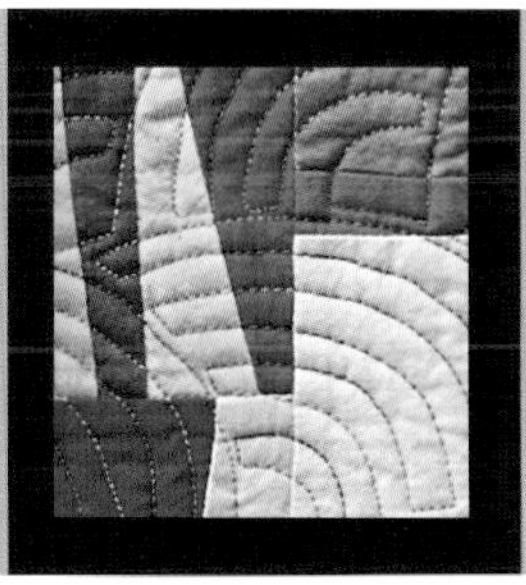

IMPROV BLOCKS

Aztec Autumn
by Cindy Grisdela
32″ × 39″, 2010

After you read this section, come back and see if you can you spot the Improv Blocks in this composition.

Improvisational Log Cabin blocks are constructed very much like a traditional Log Cabin, starting with a center square and adding strips in a clockwise or counterclockwise fashion. The difference is that the strips won't always be the same width, and some will have more than one fabric in them.

MAKING IMPROV BLOCKS

Sew all seams with the fabrics right sides together using a ¼″ seam allowance; then open and press the seams away from the center.

1. Decide on your color recipe (see Creating a Color Recipe, page 16). For this block, I'm using mostly warm reds, oranges, and browns in an analogous color scheme, with blue and purple contrasting colors for spark.

2. Begin with a 4-sided block for the center, rough cut with at least 1 edge that is angled "off-square." Using angled edges makes the finished product more interesting than if all the edges are straight.

3. Sew a strip to the right side. Trim the edges even with the center square, or add an angle to a side.

Start with a squarish center.

4. Moving counterclockwise, add another piece to the unit you just created. If the piece isn't even, all the better.

Add a strip.

5. To keep the block from looking too predictable, try adding interest by inserting an unexpected color or value. The next strip is a very narrow strip from my scrap basket, and it has a cream fabric and a smaller piece of an olive green fabric.

Add the next strip.

6. After sewing, trim the excess length before adding the next strip; then cut the unit at a gentle angle.

Trim; add the next strip.

7. After you have added the first round of strips around the center, continue adding strips for the second round using your color recipe and auditioning each strip to see if it adds interest to the emerging block. Concentrate on color, line, and pattern, evaluating your choices as you go. Too much of any single color or value becomes boring, while too many differences results in busyness.

8. The purple strip adds some visual weight to the composition, so it needs to be balanced. Adding a strip cut from a previously created strip set adds the needed weight, plus the new angled lines give some complexity to the overall design. Notice that the light tan piece on the bottom of the strip set is similar in value to the tan section added earlier. Repeating that light value forces the eye to move around the block and keeps the original light piece from becoming an oddball that creates a visual hole.

Balance the visual weights within the composition.

9. Often I add another strip set unit at right angles to the first one so the eye follows the complex line.

Another strip set adds movement.

tip

Squaring up the block as you go along isn't necessary, but you can even up the edge before adding the next strip.

10. When the block is the size you want it to be, square up the edges with a ruler and it will be ready to use in your project.

Finished block

Grape Harvest by Cindy Grisdela, 23″ × 34″, 2015

An Improv Block can be the focal point of a composition.

Photo by Gregory Staley

Block Party by Cindy Grisdela, 19″ × 23″, 2011

An oversized Improv Block combined with Inset Strips (page 59). The energy of an Anything Goes (page 22) color recipe is reduced by asymmetrical cinnamon brown borders with punchy lime green insets.

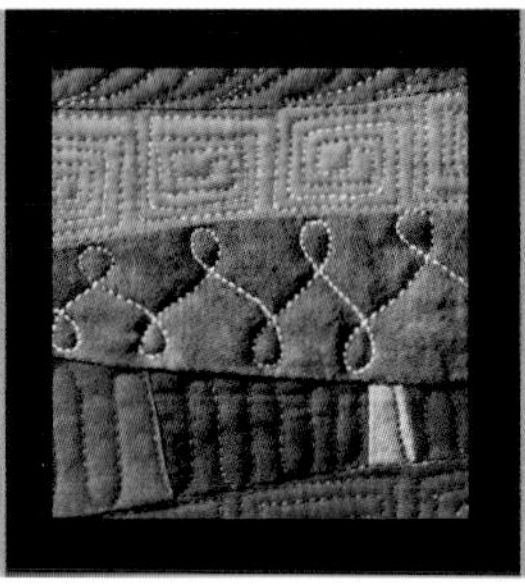

CURVED STRIPS

Painted Desert
by Cindy Grisdela
22″ × 26″, 2015

Curved Strips with Inset Strips (page 59) suggest an abstract landscape in a warm Anything Goes (page 22) color recipe calmed by blue borders.

Curved strip piecing is a versatile tool in the improvisation process. Curved Strips can be used as borders or to provide a calm resting space in an otherwise busy composition. They can also be used on their own to create abstract landscapes.

MAKING CURVED STRIPS

Sew all seams with the fabrics right sides together using a ¼″ seam allowance; then open and press the seams to one side.

1. Decide on your color recipe (see Creating a Color Recipe, page 16). For this example, I began with a cool analogous recipe of blue and green.

2. Cut your strips about 1″ wider than the finished width and about 2″ longer than the finished length.

3. Place 2 strips on your cutting surface, right sides up, with the long edges overlapping by about 1″. Using your rotary cutter, cut a gentle curving line through both layers.

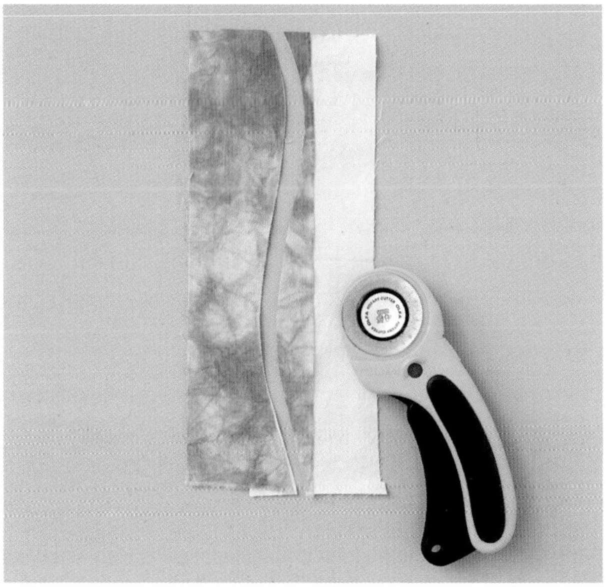

Overlap the fabrics and cut through both.

4. Remove the 2 narrow strips of excess fabric from the curve and note that the larger curved pieces fit together perfectly.

5. Sew the pieces together. When you put the 2 fabrics right sides together, it looks like they won't fit, but don't worry! It's not necessary to pin the seam, just ease the curves together gently as you sew. Aim for a ¼″ seam allowance, but it's not a problem if it's a little narrower in places. The ends won't match, but you cut them longer than you needed so you could trim the excess when the seam is finished.

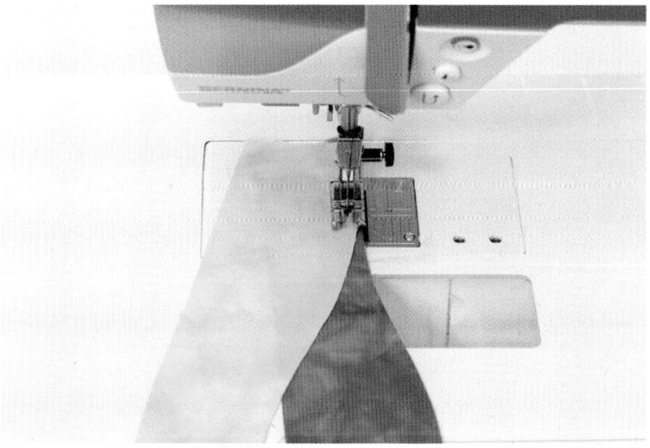

Sew carefully, right sides together.

6. Press the seam to one side. If you're using the unit as a border, you'll even up the long edges before sewing the piece to your quilt. If you're using it as part of a larger unit, use the curved edge as a guide for your next cut.

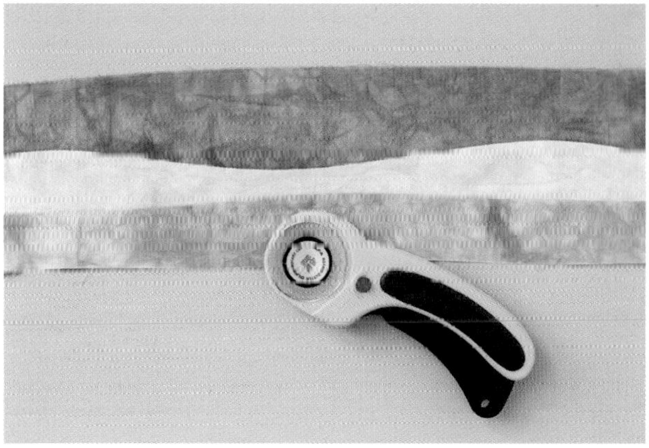

Finished curves

Intersections
by Cindy Grisdela
23″ × 37″, 2010

Curved Strip borders on two sides contain the spiky angle composition using a double complementary color recipe (page 20) of green and red and orange and blue.

Autumn Forest
by Cindy Grisdela
32″ × 39″, 2011

Curved Strips in purple and green provide a resting place for the eye in a cool analogous color recipe (page 20) with a complementary dusty pink added for the spark.

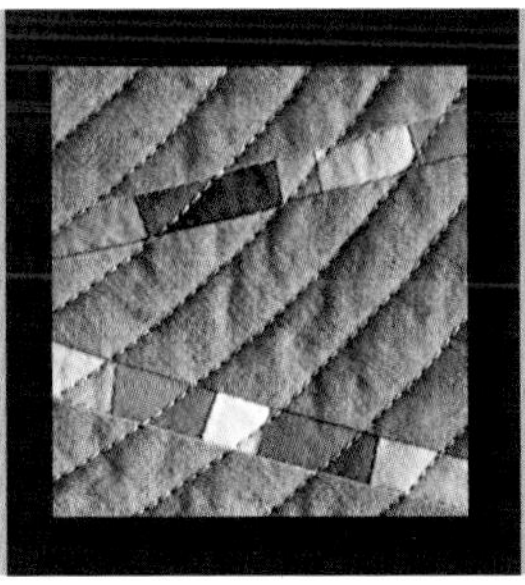

INSET STRIPS

Marbles and Chopsticks
by Cindy Grisdela
17″ × 17″, 2015

The straight lines of the Inset Strips provide contrast to the Improv Circles (page 47) in a modified monochromatic color recipe (page 18).

Inset Strips are a flexible improvisational building block. They can be used to add interest to a plain block or a splash of contrast to a block unit. You can also create a row of Inset Strip blocks for an interesting border.

Insets can be plain strips of a contrasting fabric; narrow strips cut from Angled Stripe blocks (page 43) also make great insets. I first came up with the idea for these insets after squaring up Angled Stripe blocks for a project left me with a pile of narrow strips that were too pretty to throw away.

MAKING INSET STRIPS

Sew all seams with the fabric right sides together using a ¼″ seam allowance; then press the seams toward the background.

1. Decide on your color recipe (see Creating a Color Recipe, page 16). My recipe for this exercise is a little out of my comfort zone, with several tones and shades of red in the pinks and the browns, combined with neutral taupe, tan, and beige.

2. Choose your background fabric. Depending on how many strips you intend to insert and how wide they are, the background piece should be 2″–4″ wider than the intended finished size.

3. Cut the Inset Strips from plain fabric or Angled Stripes. Insets can be any width you like. I prefer very narrow lines, so my insets are usually cut ¾″–1″ and finish at ¼″–½″.

4. Make the first cut in the background fabric, either straight or at a slight angle. I normally prefer making an angled cut, because the angle gives it more energy.

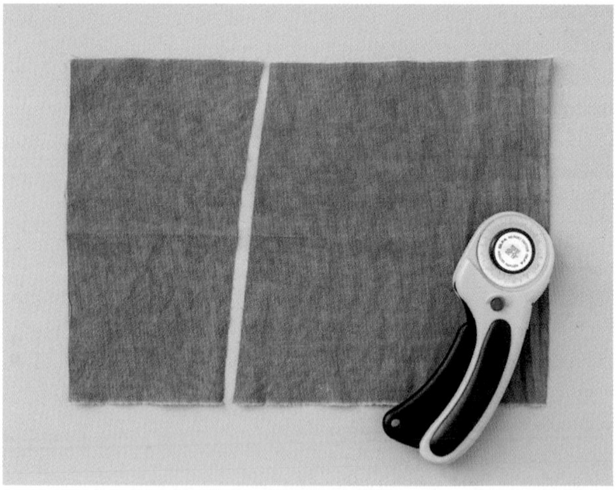

Cut the background fabric.

5. Stitch an Inset Strip to a side of the cut opening. Press toward the background fabric.

Sew the inset to one side of the opening.

6. Stitch the inset to the other cut side. Press toward the background fabric.

7. Make a second cut in the background fabric, either straight or at a slightly different angle from the first one.

8. Stitch the inset to each side of the cut opening as before. Press toward the background.

Add the second inset.

9. Continue cutting the background fabric and adding insets until you have a pleasing design for your block or border.

Time Travel
by Cindy Grisdela
30″ x 31″, 2009

Using Inset Strips, Improv Blocks (page 51), and Curved Strips (page 56) in a bright Anything Goes color recipe (page 22) creates an energetic design.

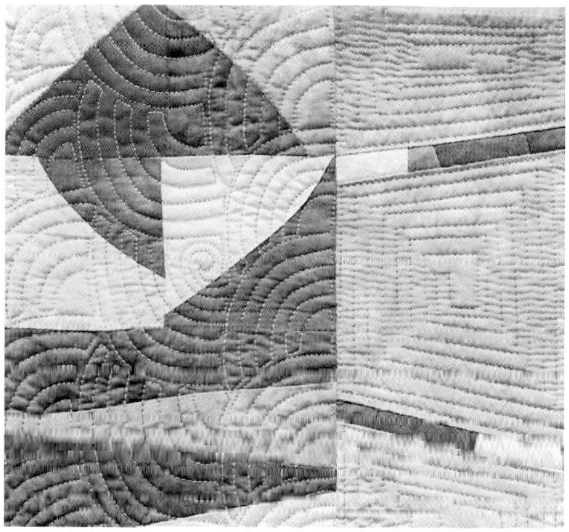

A Little Citrus
by Cindy Grisdela
25″ × 27″, 2015

Narrow Inset Strips in a wide band provide a restful but interesting space between Improv Circle (page 47) and Angled Stripe blocks (page 43) in a double complementary color recipe (page 20) of green and pink and orange and blue.

MAKING INDIVIDUAL ANGLED STRIPES

If you don't have Angled Stripes in the right color combination for a project and you don't want to create multiple blocks, you can create the strips individually.

Note: *Sew all seams with the fabric right sides together using a ¼″ seam allowance. Press the seams to one side.*

1. Cut 5 or 6 squares and rectangles in various widths with a height of at least 2″. The 2″ height gives you enough of a stripe to either cut it in half or cut gentle curves into it.

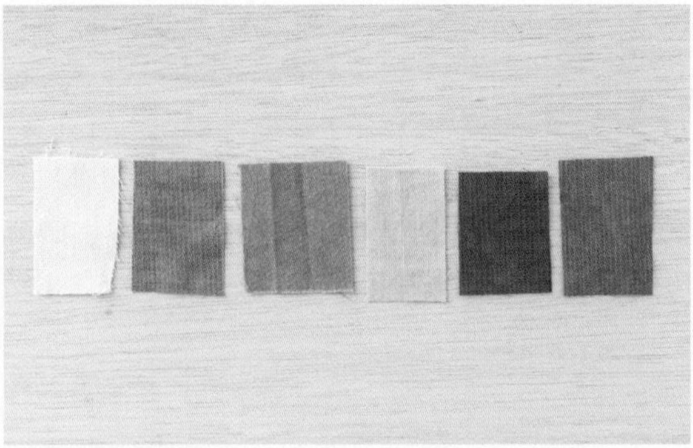

Cut individual pieces.

2. Overlap the first 2 fabrics by about ¼″ with the right sides up. Use your rotary cutter to cut an angle through both layers.

Overlap two pieces and cut.

3. Continue overlapping the fabrics and making angled cuts with the rest of the fabrics. For greater interest, each angle should be slightly different and the finished widths should vary.

Use various angles when cutting.

4. Sew the pieces together to create a strip.

Sew the pieces together.

learning to love NEGATIVE SPACE

Sunset Hills by Cindy Grisdela, 20″ × 20″, 2015

With only two design lines, this quilt is defined by its negative space.

I'll admit that when I was a traditional quiltmaker, I used to get a little nervous when presented with a pattern that had a lot of blank space. I wasn't sure what to do with all that space, how to make it part of my design, and especially how to quilt it.

But if you look at the blank space as a design element, you can turn the negative into a positive.

By definition, negative space is the open area around the forms or subjects in a composition. It can be a small area or comprise a large section of the design. Often negative space helps define the focal point of the design.

Sometimes the negative space is a small area within a block unit, as in the traditional Pinwheel block. The black negative spaces in the Pinwheel blocks help define the block shape.

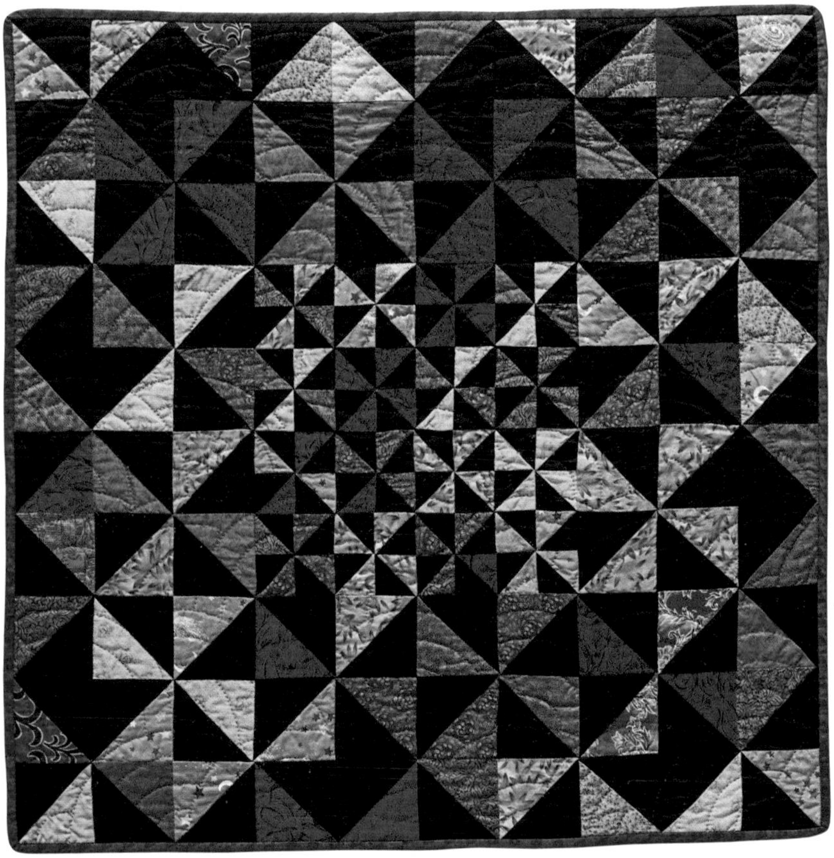

Jewel Pinwheels by Cindy Grisdela, 24″ × 24″, 2000, inspired by a pattern designed by Jean Wells

In this more traditional quilt, the black triangles (negative space) define the colorful pinwheel shapes.

CREATING BALANCE

As a design element on its own, negative space can bring balance and unity to your art quilt (see Principles of Design, page 30). These days, I use large areas of negative space often because I like the modern, minimalist look it creates. In *Spice of Life* (page 65), most of the piece is negative space. A large Improv Block (page 51) is surrounded by a narrow border that reads as negative space, so that it seems to float in the center. Then Inset Strips (page 59) made from Angled Stripes (page 43) create lines that go off in four different directions, creating open blocks (more negative space) filled with dense texture using free-motion stitching motifs. There is asymmetrical balance (page 30) in the placement of the block and the stripes. The warm analogous color recipe (page 20) of red, orange, and cinnamon includes splashes of yellow-gold to move the eye around the design.

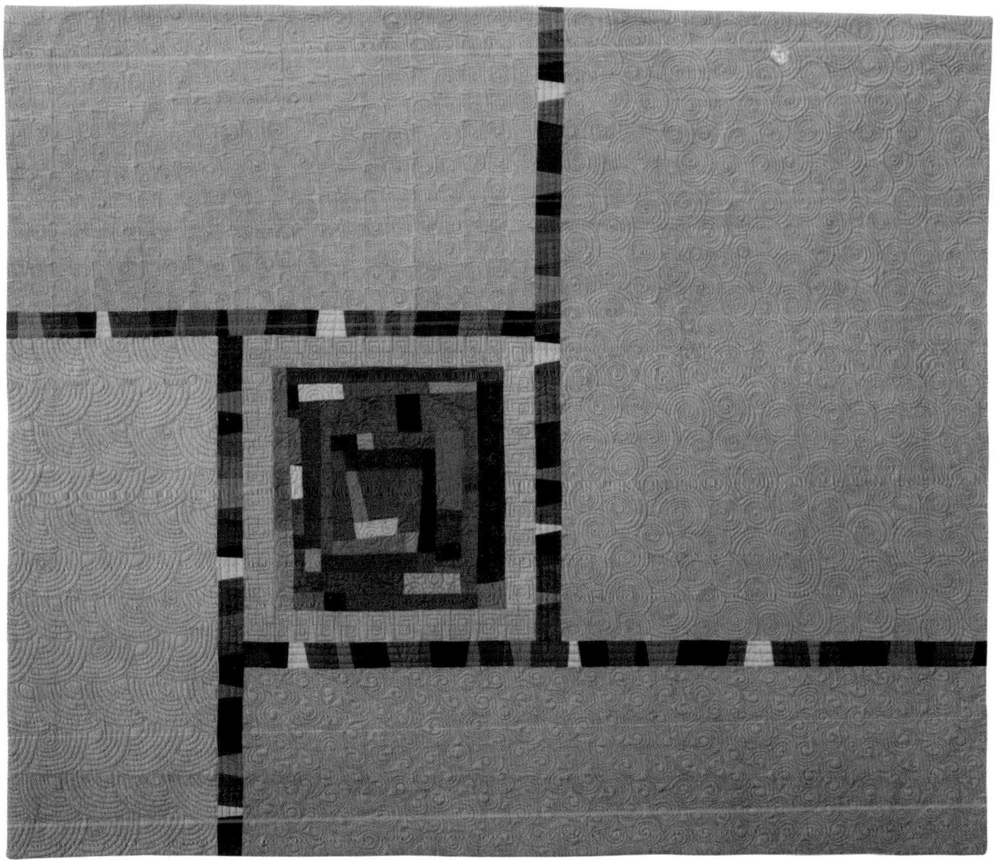

Spice of Life
by Cindy Grisdela
48″ × 41″, 2014

This quilt has large areas of negative space filled with texture from the quilting (see Quilt as Desired, page 76).

In *Midnight Sun*, the Improv Block (page 51) is again set asymmetrically in the composition, and the design is balanced by areas of negative space. The space is further defined by double cinnamon brown Inset Strips (page 59), which are also not symmetrically placed. The warm color recipe of various shades of red in the central block has accents of higher-intensity lime green and blue for interest. The contrast between the warm orange center and the complementary cool blue background draws the eye toward the focal point.

Midnight Sun
by Cindy Grisdela
20″ × 24″, 2014

The off-center focal point is balanced by the surrounding negative spaces and narrow stripes.

Contrast the composition in *Midnight Sun* (page 65) to an earlier piece, *A Walk in the Park*, where the block is closer to the center of the design and there are only single stripes, which makes the piece read sort of like a gift-wrapped package. The balance created by the negative space is very different and lacks the energy of the other two pieces, even using similar elements.

A Walk in the Park by Cindy Grisdela, 16″ × 20″, 2011

A cool blue and green color recipe, plus a more symmetrical balance of negative space, results in a more static composition.

ADDING TEXTURE

Negative space gives you the opportunity to create movement and interest in your design with texture, particularly from stitching. Taking this idea almost to an extreme, *Sunset Hills* (page 63) has only two narrow design lines and the rest of the piece is negative space. Before it was stitched, it didn't look like much. But the stitching adds movement, dimension, and texture, raising the piece to a new level, especially with the combination of spirals and pebbles in the narrow gold section. Notice also the energy created by the choice of color recipe (page 16). The dominant red gives the composition an active feeling, which is balanced by the cool green complement in the lower third of the design. The red, green, and gold of the large sections are repeated in the Angled Stripe Insets (page 59), punctuated with splashes of blue and purple.

Negative space plays a slightly different role in *Mountain Lake* (page 67). The blue and green improvisational rectangles seem to float over a background of blue, and the water concept is reinforced by the echo swirl texture that is stitched over the entire piece. The calm mood of the quilt is reflected in the analogous color recipe of cool blues and greens (page 20).

Photo by Greg R. Staley

Mountain Lake by Cindy Grisdela, 16″ × 20″, 2014

Pieced rectangles seem to float on the blue background (negative space), creating a serene mood.

Negative space can be an important tool in your design toolkit. Use it to draw attention to your focal point, add excitement to a minimalist design, or give the eye a place to rest in an otherwise busy composition.

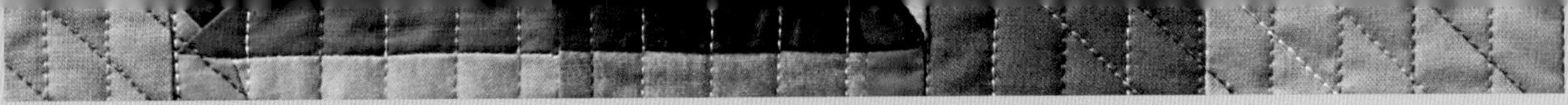

putting it all TOGETHER

Refer to Creating a Color Recipe (page 16), Elements and Principles of Design (page 24), and Building Blocks of Improv Design (page 42) as needed.

Once you have completed the exercises, what's next?

It's time to go to the design wall and start playing. Arrange the units, blocks, and pieces that you made and pick out the ones you like the best. Unless you had a specific design in mind when you were going through the exercises, usually one or more of the finished units speaks to you more than the others. You can start your original design there. Remember that you don't have to use all the units in the same quilt. See Working Improvisationally (page 36) for the process I use to put a quilt together.

If the Improv Block is your favorite, for instance, put it up on the design wall and see which of the other units work well with it. Refer to your color recipe (see Creating a Color Recipe, page 16) to decide on a dominant color.

You may need to create additional units or add background blocks or strips to fill in the design and give you space to add texture with your quilting stitches.

Ask yourself design questions as you go (see Using the Elements and Principles of Design as You Work, page 35) and don't be afraid to try a variety of settings before you decide on the final one. Don't forget to take pictures of each design before you change it, in case you want to go back to it later! There is no wrong answer.

Take a look at the quilts on the following pages to see how some of my students created their improvisational quilts.

START WITH AN IMPROV BLOCK

Notice how each of the following three quilts is completely different from the others, even though they all began with the same type of block. Improvisation allows your creativity to shine as you make your design decisions. Your personality can come through as you choose colors and shapes, so your quilt will be completely your own.

To create *Improv Orange and Green*, a quilt in warm red, orange, and yellow, Libby Samuel started with the large central Improv Block. Accents of an analogous dusky green provide the spark in the block. Then she created two smaller blocks for repetition and variety and set them in an asymmetrical balance above and below the main block. Libby used insets as a design element within her Improv Blocks, so she added Inset Strips on the left and right to create balance and unity in the composition. The green background helps tie everything together.

Improv Orange and Green by Libby Samuel, 15½″ × 26″, 2015

Start with an Improv Block.

An Improv Block also centers *Denali* by Gloria Warwick, but her composition has a very different feel. Her warm analogous color recipe uses autumn shades of russet, orange, and gold, with a gray solid and a black print for accents. Gloria's Improv Block is surrounded by Angled Stripe blocks that alternate vertically and horizontally, adding energy to the composition. She added a black print that repeats in a different place in each block, creating movement. A narrow solid border provides a resting place in the busy design, and the narrow Angled Stripe border helps contain and unify the piece. If you look closely, you'll see that Gloria added two small Improv Blocks to the outer border as well. The composition is unified and symmetrically balanced.

Denali by Gloria Warwick, 19¼″ × 19¼″, 2015

An Improv Block with Angled Stripe borders

In *Neighborhood Swatch*, Donna Marcinkowski DeSoto used a colorful Anything Goes color recipe that began with a series of Improv Blocks in the central section. Then she added black-and-white house shapes to provide a focal point in the upper third of the quilt. The addition of the black-and-white interior border was an important design decision because it adds repetition and variety and keeps the house shapes from being a hole in the composition. White can be difficult to use successfully because it draws the eye so definitively, but Donna avoided this concern by incorporating three house shapes instead of just one and by using the asymmetry of the interior border to move the eye in a different direction. The Inset Strip borders on the right and lower edges balance the black-and-white interior borders, while the Curved Strip border on the left side adds playful energy. The dark burgundy negative space helps calm the composition and gives a place for stitching to show. Random beads and sequins on the top of the piece add to the whimsical feel.

Neighborhood Swatch by Donna Marcinkowski DeSoto, 21″ × 23″, 2015

Black-and-white house shapes add whimsy to an improv design.

FOCUS ON IMPROV CIRCLES

Maybe the Improv Circles speak to you instead.

Libby Samuel began *Improv Pink and Turquoise* with Improv Circles in shades and tones of red, plus turquoise for contrast and beige as a neutral, arranging them into two vertical rows. Using the same color recipe, she stitched Angled Stripes to create a third vertical row for variety. Curved Strips and Inset Strips tie the rows together while adding interest and variety. An asymmetrical turquoise border helps unify the design.

Improv Pink and Turquoise by Libby Samuel, 26½″ × 24½″, 2015

Improv Circles take center stage.

In *Fractured*, Jeanne Coglianese got creative, adding insets to her Improv Circle blocks. She used an analogous color recipe of purple, blue, and green with pops of orange for the spark. The two Improv Circles in the upper right are balanced by the Improv Block, with insets below them. Angled Stripe units in various widths add variety and repetition, and she gave the eye a place to rest with background strips in shades of gray. The gray background acts as a neutral and allows the bright colors to shine on their own. The stitching is simple lines, but notice how the surface of the quilt is activated by a few diagonal lines in the upper right section of the piece.

Fractured by Jeanne Coglianese, 17¾″ × 20½″, 2015

Creative use of insets in Improv Circle blocks.

ACCENT A CURVED STRIP

Pat Attkisson focused on the central red Curved Strip in *Desire*. Two small red shapes help create a diagonal line from the upper left to the lower right. The red focal point is emphasized by contrasting blue rectangles on either side. Plain blocks give space to add texture with the stitching lines.

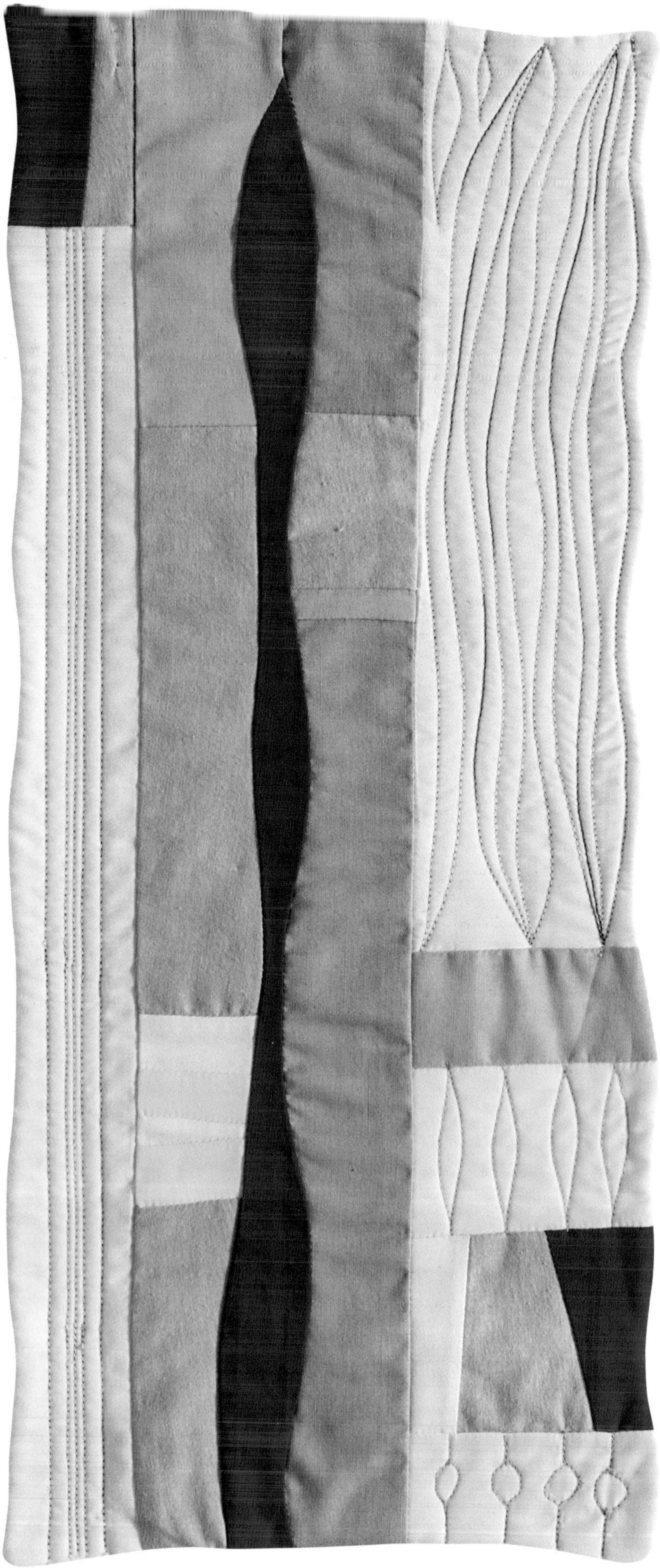

Desire
by Patricia Attkisson
8½″ × 20″, 2015

One Curved Strip is the primary focus.

Another simple yet effective composition starts with just one Angled Stripe block. Gloria Warwick was ironing fabric for her *Denali* quilt (page 69) and absentmindedly laid a single Angled Stripe block down on the ironing board with the other fabric. She was open to the "aha" moment and wondered what would happen if she created a composition with the one block surrounded by large areas of open space. *Denali #2* was born.

Gloria used the Angled Stripe unit as the focal point in the left third of the composition. She stayed with a warm color scheme of primarily orange, rust, cinnamon, and gold, with shot cottons accented by a few special patterned fabrics. Insets in different widths repeat above and below the focus block. The horizontal lines are calming, while the Angled Stripe insets add variety and help move the eye around the composition. The judicious use of one or two patterned fabrics works well here to make the simple design more visually interesting than it might have been with only solid fabrics.

Denali #2 by Gloria Warwick, 15¼″ × 25¾″, 2015

An effective design is built around just one Angled Stripe block.

In her second quilt, *Checked Out*, Jeanne Coglianese put the elements together much differently, starting with Angled Stripe units left over from her first quilt, *Fractured* (page 71). The original analogous purple, blue, and green color recipe is now more like an Anything Goes recipe, with the bright orange and yellow frame in the center pulling out the orange accents in the blocks. Jeanne successfully designed her piece with Angled Stripes, Improv Circles, and Inset Strips, plus some elements of her own, all tied together with a black-and-white check in the background. The overall effect has an active feel.

Checked Out by Jeanne Coglianese, 19¼″ × 20½″, 2015

An active Anything Goes color combination using a variety of elements

DESIGN WITH ANGLED STRIPES

Improvisational quilts don't have to be complicated. *Just Peachy* is a simple composition using only Angled Stripe blocks. Michelle Stolte decided on an analogous color recipe in tints and shades of red, orange, and yellow in mostly solids, with one cinnamon brown tone-on-tone fabric. Alternating the blocks horizontally and vertically adds energy to the design, and the brown patterned fabric helps move the eye around the composition by creating repetition and variety. The design is enhanced by Michelle's choice of angled quilting lines that intersect near the center.

Just Peachy by Michelle Stolte, 18½″ × 18½″, 2015

Stitched lines activate a simple Angled Stripes composition.

JUST INSETS

In *Improv Multi Colors*, Libby Samuel started with insets to create blocks that each explore different color combinations, some with striking contrast and others closer in value. Using an Anything Goes color recipe, she stitched some of the insets into Curved Strips to add energy to the design. The composition is balanced and unified because each block repeats the same size and design strategy, yet it is interesting and varied because each one is different in color and structure.

Improv Multi Colors by Libby Samuel, 28½″ × 28½″, 2015

Insets create a vibrant composition.

quilt AS DESIRED

"Quilt as desired" may be three of the scariest words you see in a quilt book or pattern. Many designers focus primarily on the composition of the quilt top and leave the stitching almost as an afterthought. It's sometimes difficult to know where to start. My view is that the texture created by the stitching lines can be just as important to the composition as the colors and shapes you've put into the top.

Ask yourself as you are designing your composition: What mood am I trying to convey? How can the stitching lines enhance my design? Do I want to follow the lines of the piecing or would an overall design be more desirable?

HAND STITCHING

Several of the quilts in this book are hand stitched with perle cotton thread, a big needle, and large stitches. *Jazz Rhythms* (page 10), *Time Travel* (page 33), and *Intersections* (page 58) are a few of those. Hand stitching can be a calming, meditative exercise, and it may add more of a traditional feel to the design. But it does take longer than stitching by machine.

Detail of *Jazz Rhythms* (page 10). The hand-quilted circles provide a calm secondary pattern that complements the busy, angular nature of the pieced top.

I hand quilted exclusively for many years before I felt comfortable using my sewing machine to add the texture to my work. Free-motion machine stitching takes practice. I was worried about ruining the tops that I had spent so long creating with what I considered inadequate machine stitching. But as the list of quilts I wanted to make kept getting longer and longer, I realized that I would have to make peace with my machine.

MACHINE STITCHING

I took a couple of machine quilting classes, but I don't have much patience with practice on premade quilt sandwiches just for the sake of practice. So I decided to make simple baby quilts, stitch them with a basic meander stipple, and give them away. Some I gave to my nieces and nephews and some to charity. By the time I had made six or ten of these, I was reasonably comfortable with my stippling.

It was tough to move away from that comfortable spot into more adventurous motifs. My "aha" moment came when a friend of my son's asked me to teach her how to quilt. We set a time and a date and she arrived at my studio. I had assumed that she wanted to learn the stitching part of quilting, but when we sat down at the machine, I learned that, at seventeen years old, she had never touched a sewing machine before.

So we started at the beginning and she made a simple nine-patch pillow top. After the top was finished, she said, "Now you can teach me how to quilt it." I gave her a demonstration of free-motion stitching and told her to think of her needle as a pencil and just draw with it. To my surprise, that's exactly what she did, with no hesitation! She made doodles and wrote text and even stitched an outline of a dinosaur. To be fair, she was very creative and had experience drawing with a pencil and paper. But she had no fear of the process and she didn't know what the rules were, so she just did what came naturally to her.

I realized that day that I had been letting my fear of the process hold me back. What if it wasn't good enough? What if I made a mistake?

It Won't Be Perfect

The reality is that in order to be good at machine quilting, you have to give up the idea that it will be perfect. It won't. Although you are using a machine to stitch, free-motion quilting is essentially a hand process. There will be imperfections. There will be stitches that aren't even, and maybe some that are a little wobbly. And that's okay.

As a former perfectionist, I made a deal with myself when I started machine quilting: If I think I have made a mistake when I'm stitching, I force myself to keep going, just like my mother encouraged me to do when I was practicing the piano as a child. If I can find the problem when I'm finished, then I'll consider fixing it. After all the quilting is done, I usually can't find the place I was concerned about, so it becomes part of the charm of the piece. And sometimes even if I can find the problem, fixing it would make it even more noticeable, so I opt to let it be. This approach makes the whole process a lot less intimidating.

Red Zinnia by Cindy Grisdela, 13″ × 16″, 2015

This quilt with ample negative space (page 63) is the perfect canvas for a variety of stitching motifs.

Using a Walking Foot

A walking foot attachment on your machine allows you to stitch straight or gently wavy lines on your quilt. The walking foot helps keep even feed on both the top and bottom of your quilt sandwich.

To create horizontal or vertical lines, use blue painter's tape or a light chalk line to mark the first line. If you choose to use a marking tool, test it first in an inconspicuous area to make sure the mark will disappear after stitching. Then you can line up the first stitched line with an edge on the presser foot to set the spacing for the next line, and continue the design. Consider varying the width of the lines to create a less symmetrical, more visually appealing grid. Horizontal or vertical lines, or both, are often appropriate when your design is very busy or contains many curved elements.

Box of Marbles by Cindy Grisdela, 16″ × 20″, 2011

Horizontal and vertical stitching lines contrast with the curved piecing.

Gently curving lines can also be stitched effectively with a walking foot. Mark or stitch the first line freehand; then stitch the rest of the lines based on that first line by using the edge of your walking foot as a guide.

Autumn Stripes by Cindy Grisdela, 17″ × 37″, 2013

Gently waving stitched lines add a calm and graceful feel.

A walking foot is useful for stitching organic lines too. You can draw them first if you like, or simply guide the machine to stitch the lines freehand.

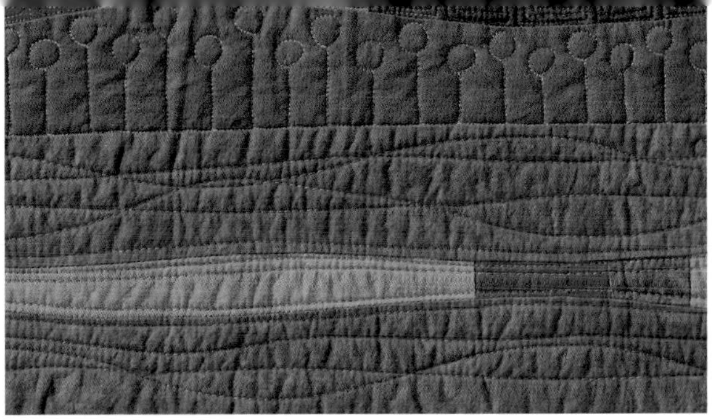

Detail of *Painted Desert* (page 30). A walking foot can be used for organic, free-form lines.

A large spiral is often an effective way to add texture to a smaller piece. Starting from the inside, stitch a spiral shape and echo it all the way around. You may have to begin by marking the line and stitching it with a darning foot, since the walking foot doesn't do well making tight turns. Once you get to the point where the walking foot is usable, align the edge of the foot against the stitched line to keep the spacing even.

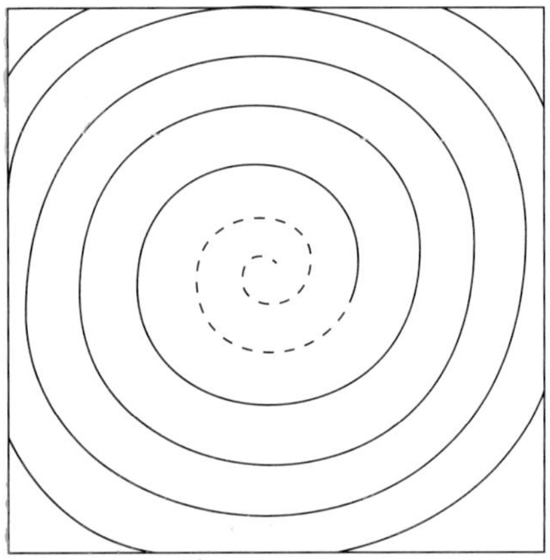

You might need to start with free-motion when stitching a large spiral.

Marbles and Chopsticks by Cindy Grisdela, 17″ × 17″, 2015

A large stitched spiral creates texture.

Free-Motion Stitching

You don't need a special sewing machine to free-motion quilt. I create all my quilts on a regular home BERNINA 1080 machine that I've had for more than fifteen years.

You do need an open-toe or darning foot for your machine and the ability to lower or cover the feed dogs that normally grasp the fabric from the bottom. The open-toe foot doesn't put any pressure on the top of the quilt, and with the feed dogs down or covered there's no pressure on the bottom either. So all your machine is doing is moving the needle up and down. This gives you the freedom to move the quilt and stitch in any direction—forward, backward, or sideways—using the needle to draw the motifs you choose.

You control the speed of the machine with your foot on the pedal and the speed of your stitching with your hands on the quilt. If your machine is too fast and your hands too slow, you'll end up with tiny, cramped stitches. If the machine is too slow, you might have stitches of widely varying lengths. It's a Goldilocks compromise that will be different for each person—not too fast, not too slow, but just right for you.

Collection of my favorite free-motion stitching motifs

tip

Buy inexpensive squares of felt to practice your free-motion stitching. Stack two pieces together to mimic the quilt sandwich and try each new stitch pattern on a different color of felt. You can keep the felt squares to remind you of your progress and to keep track of your favorite designs.

Stipple Stitch

Many quilters begin learning free-motion stitching with a meander or stipple stitch. It looks a bit like a jigsaw puzzle piece and curves gently in an allover pattern that works well on busy quilts.

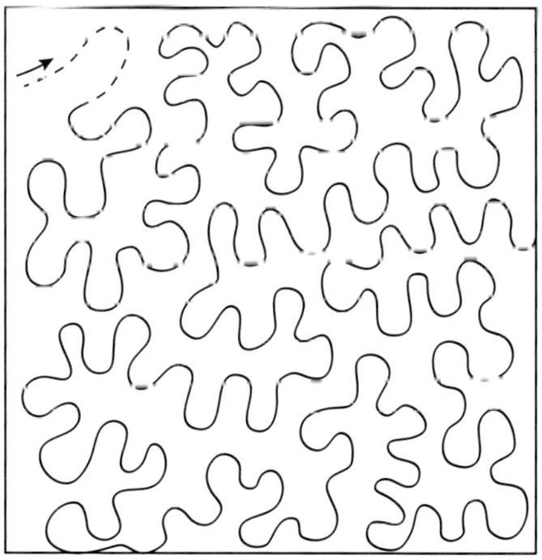

Stipple stitching

Pebble or Bubble Stitch

One of my favorite free-motion stitches is the pebble or bubble stitch. This one takes some time to execute, but the texture it provides is so interesting that it's worth it to me. To start, simply stitch a circle, then stitch another one next to it, and continue until you have filled the space. In order to nest the circles together, you will need to stitch over your previous stitching sometimes. Aim for circles of different sizes to emphasize the texture.

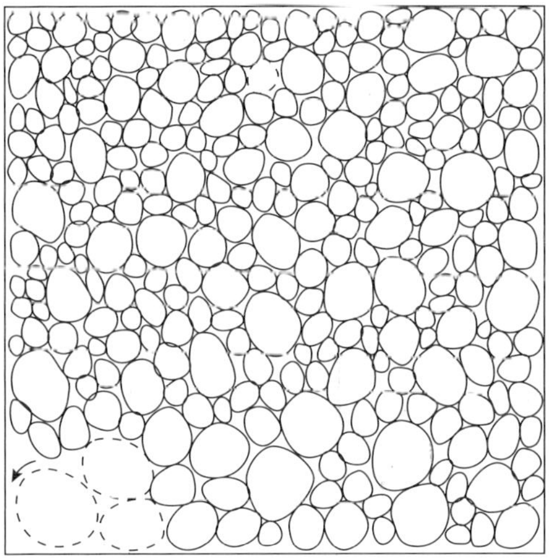

Pebble stitching

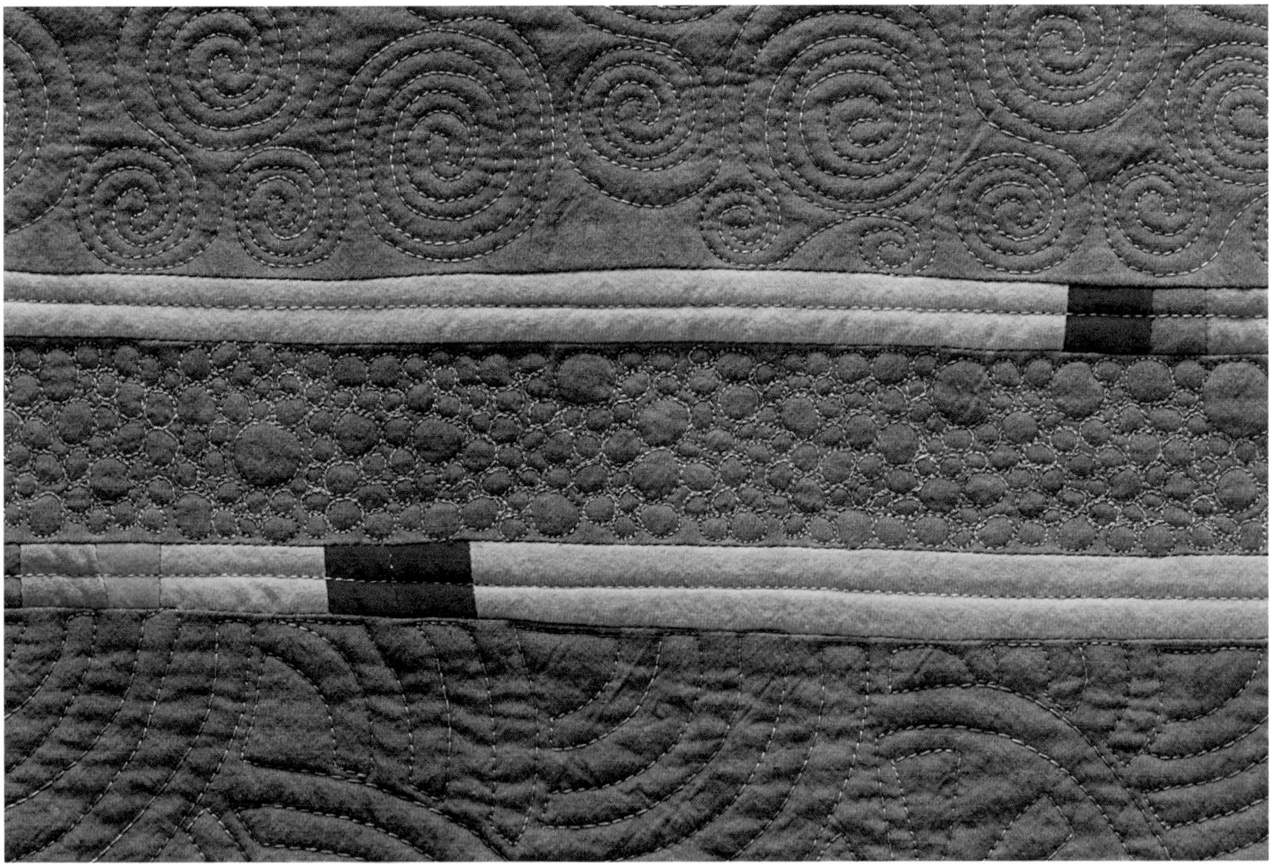

Detail of *Through the Window* (page 36). Pebble stitching is the perfect stitch for filling this narrow area.

Spirals

Spirals are a versatile free-motion motif. They can be open or closed, round or square. For an open spiral, simply stitch the spiral from the outside to the inside; then cross over the lines to get out and start another one. You'll have to let go of the "rule" that quilting lines should never cross for this one, though.

To make a closed spiral, you'll need to leave enough room going into the spiral to come back out again. This motif can be stitched with the spirals close together so they seem to nest beside each other, or it can be more open. This is a good background filler option.

Round spiral stitching

You can make your spirals square by stitching angles instead of curves. They can be open or closed too.

Square spiral stitching

Details of *Midnight Sun* (page 65). Open and closed spiral stitching

Seashells

Seashells are another good filler motif. Stitch a tear-shaped loop and then reverse direction and echo stitch around it once or twice before starting another one.

Seashell stitching

Detail of *Wild Geese in Flight* (page 6). Seashell stitching on the left

Fans

Fans are another of my favorite motifs to stitch. They work best to fill a large area, or as an overall design for a small piece. Beginning at one edge of the area to be filled, stitch a curved shape that goes from one side to the other. Pivot and make a few stitches; then pivot and echo the curved shape to the other side. Repeat for two or three echoes and then begin another fan. Fans are usually stitched in rows and nested against each other, but you can also stitch them randomly for a different look. Also consider adding spirals or some other element to add interest.

Fan stitching

Detail of *Spice of Life* (page 65). Fan stitching and open square and circle spirals

Waves

Recently I've started using a wave design on some of my quilts. First stitch gently curving lines about 1″–2″ apart, using a walking foot. Then, using a darning foot, go back and free-motion stitch crescent shapes that bounce from one line to the other. In the next section, make the crescents go the other way.

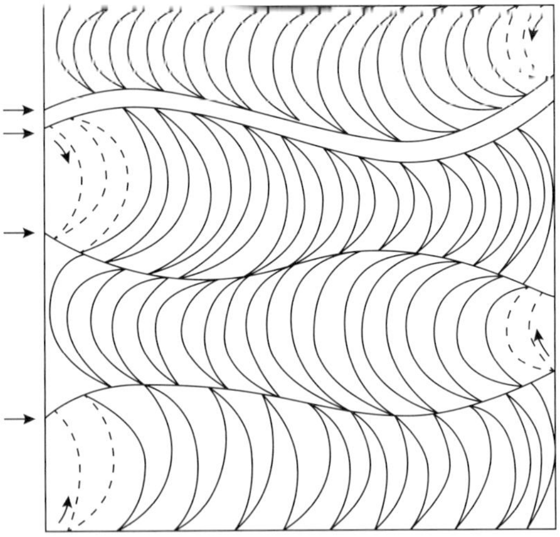

Wave stitching

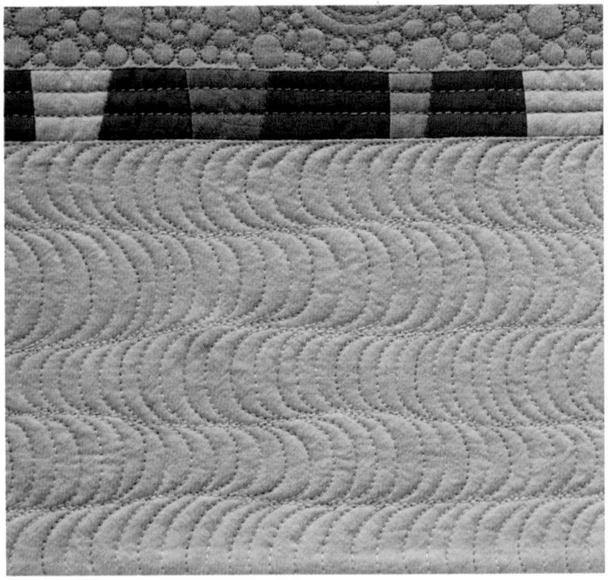

Detail of *Sunset Hills* (page 31). Variegated thread adds interest to the wave stitching.

Combining Motifs

Many free-motion stitching motifs lend themselves to combinations, particularly spirals. Consider spirals with stippling, or spirals with pebbles.

Spiral and stipple stitch combination

Detail of *Wild Geese in Flight* (page 6). Spiral and stipple stitch combination

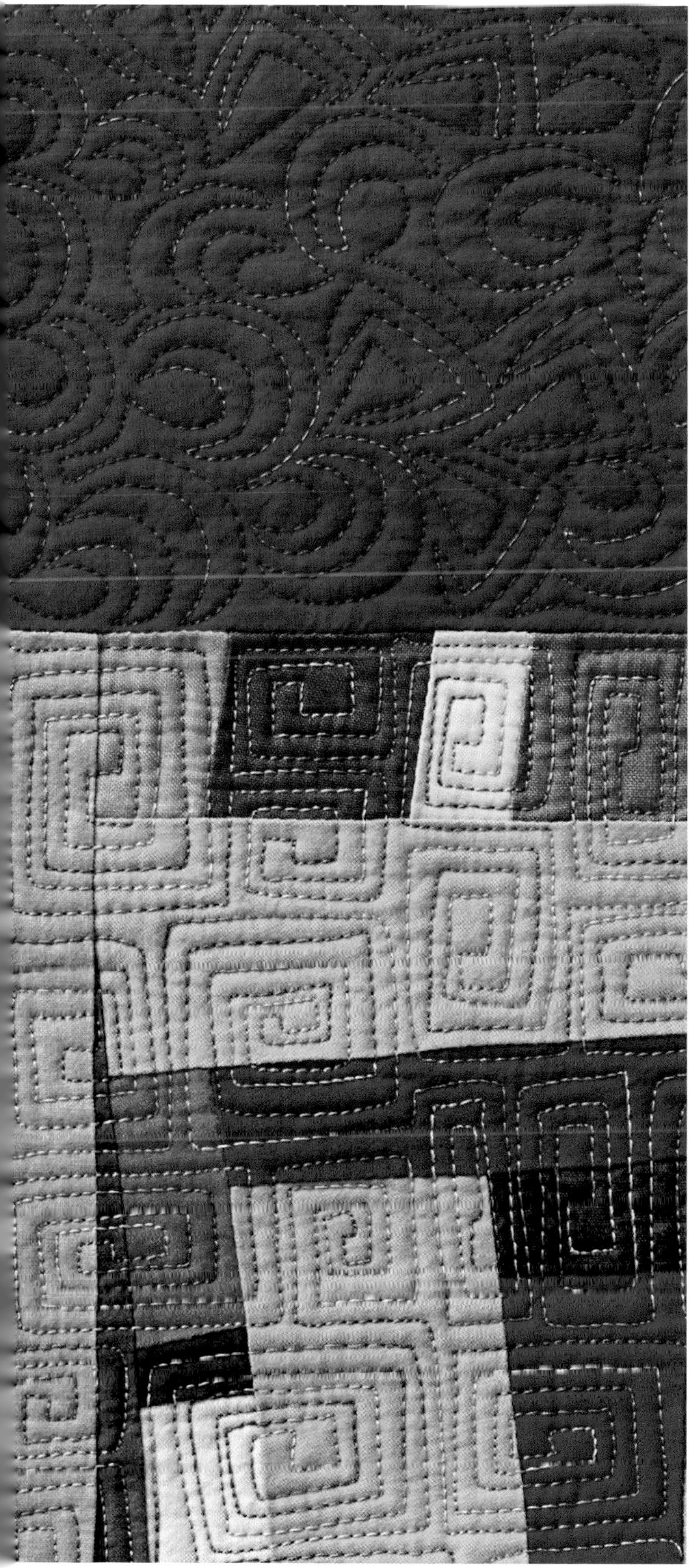

Detail of *Red Totem* (page 4). Square spiral stitching and combination seashell stitching

To add interest to seashells, vary the shape into a flame or an elongated triangle. I like to use an odd number of these elements in groupings of three or five before going back to the seashell shape.

Seashell stitch variation with flames

Use your imagination to come up with other ideas. Check the Internet for books, magazines, and tutorials on quilting and quilting designs.

tip

I use 3″ × 3″ squares of rubber rug backing material to move my quilt when I'm stitching, as an alternative to gloves. Place the squares on top of the piece and rest your fingertips gently on the squares to give you more control as you stitch.

Remember to relax when you're stitching. If you feel your shoulders hunching up around your ears, it's time to take a break! It's a good idea to start with smaller projects, such as pillow tops, place mats, or table runners, to help you become comfortable with the free-motion process.

A WORD ABOUT THREAD

Top Thread

I use variegated thread for all my quilts because I like the way it enhances the depth and dimension of the texture in the stitching of the quilt. My favorite is King Tut (from Superior Threads) for the top thread because it comes in so many wonderful color combinations.

Some quilts call for threads with every color of the rainbow in them, usually because the quilt itself is busy. Others need a more subtle approach, where the thread is variegated only across a narrow range of one color.

If you use a highly variegated thread on a solid fabric, the surface may read differently than you intended because of the way the color variations in the thread show on the solid. This effect is very apparent in *Building Blocks*, where the blue sections of thread recede into the blue of the background, while the yellow sections stand out. There's nothing wrong with this effect, as long as it's what you want to convey.

Bobbin Thread

King Tut is 40-weight thread; for the bobbin thread, I like to use a 50-weight thread that is thinner so it is less likely to show through on the top. I usually use MasterPiece (also from Superior Threads) in the bobbin in a color that blends with the top thread.

For free-motion quilting instruction and inspiration, see Resources (page 95).

Building Blocks
by Cindy Grisdela
18″ × 22″, 2010

The highly variegated thread enhances the depth and dimension of the texture on the solid background

finishing TOUCHES

Cornflower Blues by Cindy Grisdela, 12″ × 9″, 2015

The quilt is attached to a painted black canvas.

When your improvisational art quilt is finished, you need to decide what to do about the raw edges and how you are going to present it.

TO BIND OR NOT TO BIND?

The traditional way to finish the edges of a quilt is with a narrow binding that either blends with the top or creates a contrasting line at the edge. For many, the binding defines the piece as a quilt rather than a piece of art, so you need to decide if your design will be enhanced by a binding or if you want to finish the edges another way. Even some nontraditional pieces need a contrasting line at the edge for definition.

If the binding line isn't necessary as a design element, there are other finishing options for an art quilt that will hang on the wall and isn't meant to be used.

Green Marbles
by Cindy Grisdela
14″ × 43″, 2012

The red traditional binding provides a complementary contrast to the green background and ties in with the red in the blocks.

FACINGS

Pillowcase-Style Facing

The easiest way to finish the edges of your quilt is a pillowcase-style facing with a keyhole opening. This works best on smaller pieces.

Back of *Autumn Forest* (page 46), showing a pillowcase-style facing

1. If your piece is meant to have straight edges, square it up with a square ruler and a straightedge.

2. Cut a piece of fabric the same size as the finished quilt. Try to match the fabric as much as possible to the color used on the outer edges of the front.

3. Place the facing fabric, right sides together, on the front of the quilt. Sew around all the edges with a ¼″ seam. Clip the corners.

4. Using blunt-nosed scissors, carefully cut a slit in the facing fabric without catching the quilt top.

After stitching, carefully cut a slit in the back to turn the facing right side out.

5. Clip corners and turn the quilt right side out. Press the edges of the facing flat, creating a knife-edge seam.

6. Carefully trim an oval keyhole shape out of the facing fabric on the back, leaving about a 3″–4″ border on all sides.

7. Press under ¼″ on the cut edge and hand stitch it to the back of the quilt.

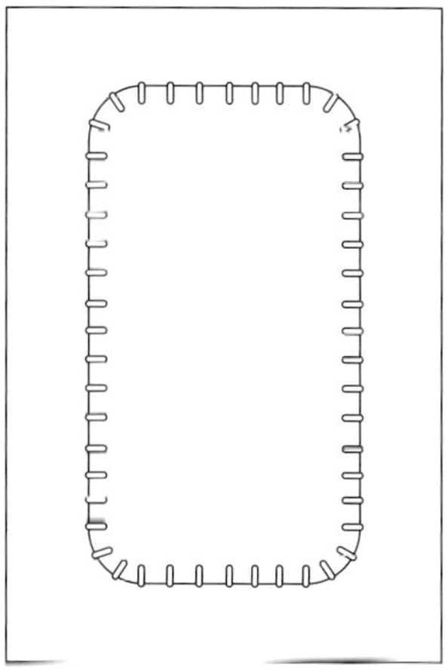

After ironing the facing to the back, cut a keyhole shape out of the facing fabric. Turn under and hand stitch the facing down.

Frame Facing

For larger pieces, a custom facing may be preferable so you don't need as much fabric.

This style of facing is made using strips that form a frame on the back of the quilt.

1. If your quilt is meant to have straight edges, square it up with a square ruler and straightedge.

2. Cut 2 strips 2½″ × the width of the shorter sides of the quilt. Press under ¼″ on the long edges to create a finished edge that you will hand stitch down at the end.

3. To fit your frame exactly to the quilt, place the strips along the short sides of the quilt, right sides together and edges aligned so the fold is on the inside away from the edge. You won't stitch anything down until the frame is completed, but laying the frame strips on top of the quilt while you're constructing the frame helps ensure that everything will fit together properly in the end.

4. Measure the longer sides of the quilt from the folded edge of one short frame strip to the folded edge of the other strip and add ½″ for seam allowances. Lay the long strip on the quilt to double-check the fit before stitching—in case your fold is not quite ¼″. Adjust the fit if necessary.

The ends of the long strips should overlap the folded edge on the short strips. Cut 2 strips this measurement and then press under ¼″ on a long edge of each of the longer strips.

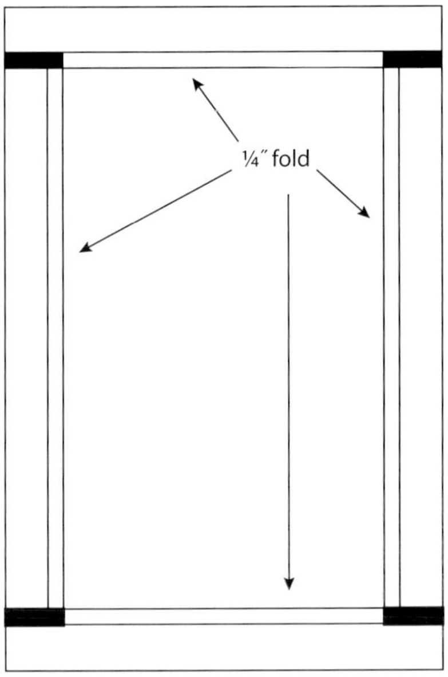

Press under ¼″ on the frame strips. You will hand stitch these edges to the back of the quilt after the frame is sewn on. The ends of the long strips should overlap the folded edge on the short strips (areas in back).

5. Open up the fold on a short side and match the top raw edge of the long side to the raw edge of the open fold on the short side, right sides together. Make sure the fold of the long edge is on the inside and the raw edges match on the sides.

6. Stitch along the open fold line just to the width of the long strip, keeping the fold on the long side folded closed. Press toward the fold on the short side.

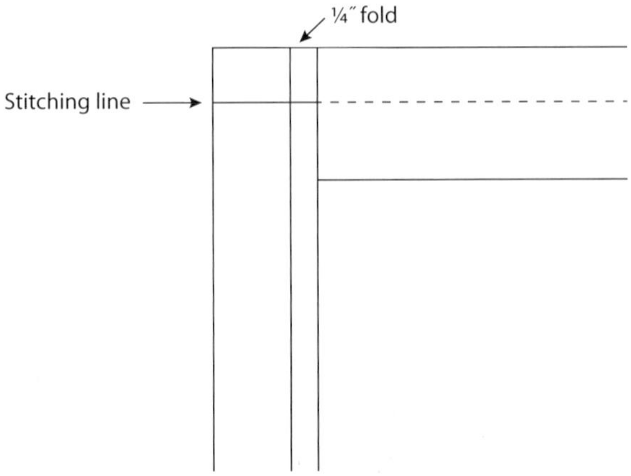

Match the short raw edge of the long sides to the upper raw edge of the fold on the short sides. Press toward the fold on the short side.

7. Repeat for the other corners, creating your custom frame.

8. Place the frame on the front of the quilt, right sides together. Pin and stitch through all the layers using a ¼″ seam. It may help to use a walking foot attachment if you have one. Clip the corners.

9. Turn the facing to the back of the quilt. Use a chopstick or other pointed object to carefully push out the corners. Press the facing to the back so the seam lies flat.

10. Pin the facing in place and hand stitch the folded edges to the back of the quilt.

Back of *Spice of Life* (page 65), showing a frame facing

DEALING WITH IRREGULAR EDGES

Sometimes your vision calls for a quilt that doesn't have straight edges. Edges can be curved, irregular, or perhaps a combination of the two.

Facings will still work in these cases. If the quilt is on the smaller side, a pillowcase finish (page 91) might be the way to go. You'll need to stitch the backing to the quilt from the quilt side, rather than from the backing side, so you can follow the edge correctly.

The back of *Time Travel* (page 33) has gently curved edges, and a pillowcase facing with a keyhole opening worked just fine.

If the quilt is larger and you need to create a frame facing, simply add another inch or two to the width of the facing frame to accommodate the irregularities. *Jazz Rhythms* (page 10) has irregular edges to go with the jazz nature of the piece. A wider facing will accommodate an assortment of irregular edges; stitch from the quilt side along the irregular edge and be sure to trim any excess facing fabric before you turn it to the back. The width of the facing that shows on the back varies accordingly.

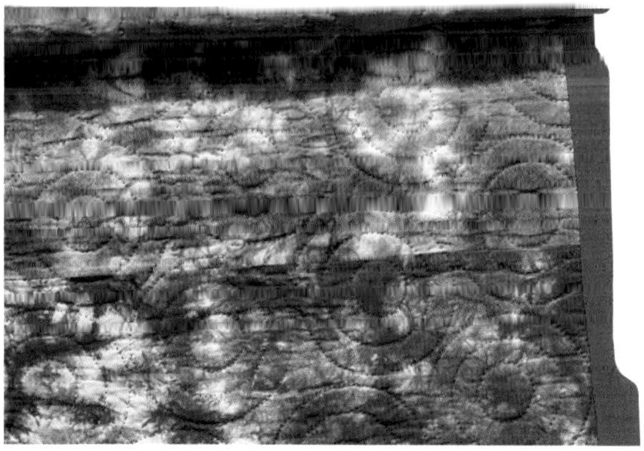

The back facing on *Jazz Rhythms* (page 10) varies in width because of the irregular edges on the quilt.

ALTERNATIVES TO SLEEVE AND SLAT HANGING

Art quilts often require different hanging treatment than traditional quilts. While larger quilts usually are fine with a sleeve on the back and a slat or dowel to hang on nails in the wall, smaller pieces may benefit from a more artistic presentation.

Framing

One approach is to frame your work. Framing gives the piece a professional finish that announces that your quilt is intended to be art. The negative to this option is that it may require the services of a professional framer, which can add a significant cost. I have gone this route for some of my art quilts, with very nice results.

Charmed Zebra by Cindy Grisdela, 14″ × 15″, 2008

This quilt was professionally framed.

Mounting on Canvas

What if you don't want to spend all that time and money? I share studio space with nine other artists, including painters and photographers. I'm the only fiber artist there. Several years ago I was chatting with my painter friends about how to present my smaller pieces, and they encouraged me to try mounting my art quilts on stretched canvas.

This is an easier, more economical solution that has been very popular with visitors and collectors of my work. It does, however, restrict me to working in more standard sizes so my art quilts will fit on the canvases. I have to consider what size the finished piece will be before I get too far into the design if it's meant to be presented in this way.

The size restriction can be a positive as well. The pieces mounted on canvas can be presented in small groupings because they are all the same size, or sizes can be mixed and matched successfully.

Photo by Cindy Grisdela

Grouping of 12″ × 12″ art quilts over a bookcase

To mount your small art quilt on canvas, follow these steps:

Prestretched artist canvas painted with black acrylic paint

1. Paint a prestretched artist canvas with black acrylic paint on the sides and about 1″ onto the front.

2. Finish your art quilt about ½″ smaller than the canvas top, using a black facing fabric and a pillowcase finish (page 91). There's no need to cut the keyhole and hand stitch it to the back because the back will be attached to the canvas and it won't show.

3. After the paint has dried and the quilt is faced, apply a thin layer of gel medium to the canvas front and carefully place the quilt on top, aligning the edges.

4. Press down on the edges to press out any excess medium. Carefully wipe away any excess with a paper towel. You don't want the gel medium to dry on the outside of the canvas because it isn't invisible.

5. Cover the quilt with wax paper and weight it with books or a piece of plywood for at least several hours, preferably overnight.

6. After the piece has dried, attach hooks and hanging wire to the back.

If you use one of these finishing methods, you'll never again be asked why you're hanging potholders on the wall!

ABOUT THE AUTHOR

Photo by Liz Cezat

Cindy Grisdela is an award-winning fiber artist with over 30 years' experience creating eye-catching quilts. From her studio overlooking a lake in Reston, Virginia, Cindy draws inspiration for her contemporary quilts from the colors and textures she sees outside her window every day, from the pebbles on the path and currents in water to the colors of a meadow. She is fascinated with color and likes to use fabric the way a painter might use paint.

Cindy's work has evolved over the years from her start as a traditional quiltmaker to a more unique, modern style. Not knowing exactly how a design is going to turn out before she starts is one of her favorite parts of the improvisational process. Anything can happen, and that's exciting. She encourages her students to embrace the process and let go of the rules to discover their inner creativity.

Cindy travels extensively, showing and selling her work at well-known events, including the American Craft Council Show in Baltimore, the Northern Virginia Fine Arts Festival, the Palm Beach Fine Craft Show, the Chicago One of a Kind Show, and the Washington Craft Show. Her quilting designs have been published in books and magazines.

For more information, visit Cindy's website and blog at cindygrisdela.com or follow her on Instagram @cindygrisdelaquilts.

RESOURCES

Free-Motion Quilting

Books:

Beginner's Guide to Free-Motion Quilting by Natalia Bonner (Stash Books)

First Steps to Free-Motion Quilting by Christina Cameli (Stash Books)

Free-Motion Quilting with Angela Walters by Angela Walters (Stash Books)

Modern Quilting Designs by Bethany Pease (Stash Books)

Shape by Shape Free-Motion Quilting with Angela Walters by Angela Walters (Stash Books)

Blog:

The Free-Motion Quilting Project by Leah Day (freemotionquilting.blogspot.com)